INTREPID

James Taylor

Iceland

Hardie Grant

EXPLORE

Intrepid

WHAT MAKES AN INTREPID GUIDE

Intrepid, for us, means being adventurous, brave and, above all, curious. Whether you're trekking through remote countryside or trying a new-to-you dish, these kinds of experiences allow us to reach beyond our everyday to learn something new and connect with people and places.

Intrepid Guides are for the intrepid traveller – those who want to see the world in meaningful and memorable ways, rather than just push through a to-do list.

Each guide highlights places, activities and experiences that make a country special and allow us to connect to these destinations and gain life-long memories and broaden our perspective.

The contents of this guide align with everything that drives Intrepid Travel and Hardie Grant Explore – chasing adventure in new (to us) places while getting to know the people who call them home and supporting their communities along the way.

INTREPID

Iceland

ACTIVITIES & SPORTS
129

HISTORY
157

ART & CULTURE
181

ARCHIT-ECTURE
191

SLOW TRAVEL
201

✱ INTRODUCING INTREPID TRAVEL

As the world's largest purpose-led adventure travel company, Intrepid Travel has been taking travellers around the globe since 1989.

On hundreds of trips in over 100 countries, Intrepid brings small groups of like-minded travellers together with a locally based leader. Intrepid itineraries weave the highlights into the hard-to-forget moments in hard-to-find places. From homestays to Indigenous community-led experiences, between the hidden noodle bars and backstreet bodegas, Intrepid experiences are built to keep the economic benefits of travel where they belong.

It all stems from a simple mission: create positive change through the joy of travel. As a B Corp, Intrepid is committed to balancing purpose and profit by operating equitably, sustainably and transparently. The Intrepid Foundation, established in 2002, gives travellers a way to give back to the places they've visited, by supporting organisations around the world that are making a difference in their communities.

At Intrepid, travel is about more than just seeing the world, it's about experiencing it and sparking connections with Intrepid people wherever you go.

Learn more at intrepidtravel.com.

INTRODUCTION

Having spent years living in Iceland, and many more returning for travel, work and family, I'm still blown away by just how much the country has affected me. The cataclysm of steaming geothermal energy, emerald-green canyons, volcanoes, glaciers and rushing waterfalls combine to create one of the best travel destinations on Earth.

Embarking on a journey in Iceland is akin to stepping through a portal to a different realm, where you'll feel things you've never felt before. What is it about Iceland that makes it so alluring that it has travellers falling in love before even stepping off the plane? Indeed, it's the untamed and formidable forces of nature, the breathtaking views that unfold at every turn and the enduring spirit and traditions of the Icelandic people. But it's also more than that.

For me, the big reason Iceland has captured the imagination of travellers around the world is the country's relationship with time itself. Iceland is one of Earth's youngest land masses, born from fiery volcanos and the shifting of tectonic plates over millennia, long after the major continents had found their places. Counterintuitively, this makes Iceland feel ancient to us, and to explore it is like tapping into a profound, shared memory of our planet as it once was.

In this place where the thread of time twitches differently, it's easy to feel as if you've been transported to another era, a witness to geological wonders that shaped our home countries as we know them today. All of this is to say that Iceland is a country guaranteed to leave you in a state of wonder. Shimmering fjords, rushing waterfalls, brooding volcanoes and steaming hot springs are just the beginning. The addictive feeling of being alone in a vast and untouched natural landscape is what travel in Iceland is all about, and it's a feeling that many of us ache for all our lives. Iceland is our remedy – ready to dive in?

James Taylor

DENMARK STRAIT

ICELAND SEA

Drangajökull

SKAGI

Ísafjörður
Súðavík
Flateyri

Húnaflói

Þingeyri

▲ *Kaldbakur*

Hólmavík

VATNSNES

Patreksfjörður

Blönduós

Brjánslækur

Reykhólar

Breiðafjörður

Borðeyri

Stykkishólmur
Hvammsfjörður
Búðardalur

Ólafsvík
Grundarfjörður
SNÆFELLSNES

Snæfellsjökull ▲

Bifröst

Arnarstapi

Hafffjörður

Kleppjárnsreykir

Langjökull

Borgarnes

Faxaflói

Þvottahellir
^

Akranes

Gullfoss ⫿

REYKJAVÍK ◉
Mosfellsbær
Flúðir

Garður

Keflavík
Hveragerði
Selfoss

REYKJANES
Hella

▲ *Sýlingarfell*
Grindavík
Þorlákshöfn

ICELAND

Capital city: Reykjavík

Official language: Icelandic

A volcanic island, home to approximately 200 volcanoes, but only 30–40 are active

11 per cent of the country is covered in glaciers

NORTH ATLANTIC OCEAN

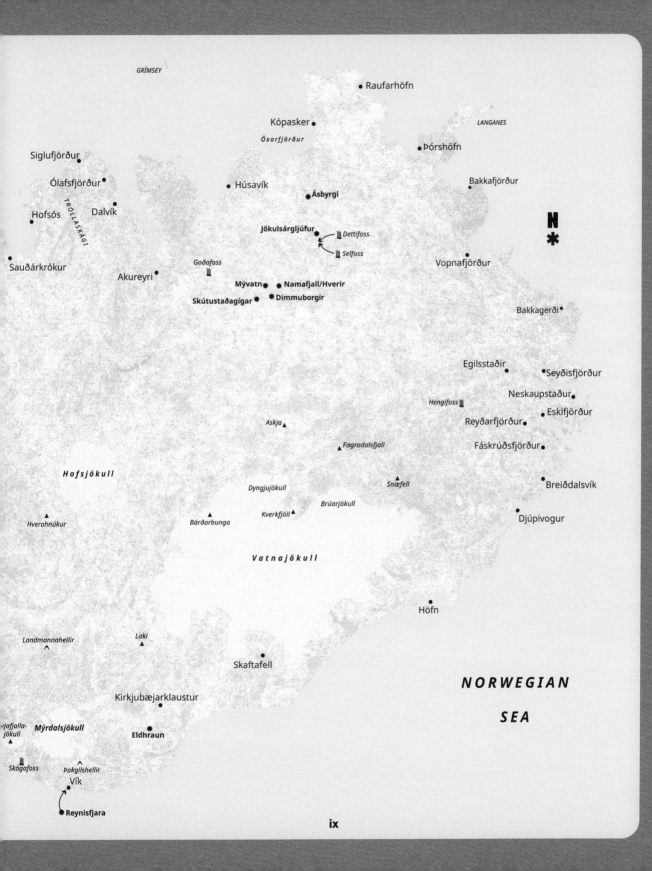

GRÍMSEY

Raufarhöfn

Kópasker

LANGANES

Öxarfjörður

Þórshöfn

Siglufjörður

Ólafsfjörður

Húsavík

Ásbyrgi

Bakkafjörður

Hofsós

TRÖLLASKAGI

Dalvík

Jökulsárgljúfur ⫘ Dettifoss

Sauðárkrókur

Goðafoss

⫘ Selfoss

Vopnafjörður

Akureyri

Mývatn ✳ ✳ Namafjall/Hverir

N

✳

Skútustaðagígar ✳ ✳ Dimmuborgir

Bakkagerði

Egilsstaðir

Seyðisfjörður

Neskaupstaður

Hengifoss ⫘

Eskifjörður

Reyðarfjörður

Fáskrúðsfjörður

Askja ▲

Fagradalsfjall ▲

Hofsjökull

Dyngjujökull

Snæfell ▲

Breiðdalsvík

Brúarjökull

Hverahnúkur ▲

Bárðarbunga ▲

Kverkfjöll ▲

Djúpivogur

Vatnajökull

Höfn

Landmannahellir ⌃

Laki ▲

Skaftafell

Kirkjubæjarklaustur

NORWEGIAN

SEA

...jafjalla-
jökull ▲

Mýrdalsjökull

Eldhraun ✳

Skógafoss ⫘

Þakgilshellir ⌃

Vík

✳ Reynisfjara

THE BASICS

History

Iceland has an incredible and well-recorded history that can be traced back to the ninth century when the first Vikings settled on the island in the year 874. Most, if not all, of the significant events in Iceland's settlement history are recorded in two significant works of literature. The first is the *Íslendingabók* (The Book of Icelanders), a historical narrative of Iceland beginning with the arrival of Irish monks in the ninth century, followed by the arrival of the first Viking settlers, the establishment of Iceland's Alþing in 930 and the adoption of Christianity in 1000. The second work of literature that details the early days is the Icelandic Sagas, a collection of long narrative stories based on the historical events of the early days of Iceland's settlement. There's a focus on history, but the Sagas also delve more into the characters of the time, detailing adventures, family feuds, romance, travels and other significant events. They're based on the tradition of oral storytelling, a tradition that kept the early settlers entertained on those dark winter days, which explains why some of the Sagas are embellished to the point of fantasy.

Discovery

The first recorded mention of Iceland was from the Greek explorer named Pytheas, who mentioned an island in a frozen sea, six days north via ship from Britain. The first Norseman to arrive was Naddodur the Viking, who was blown off course by a storm while sailing back to Norway from the Faroe Islands in the year 861 CE. After washing up on the east coast of Iceland, he climbed the nearest mountain, declared the island uninhabited, named it Snowland and sailed home. Then came the Swedish Viking Garðar Svavarsson, also blown off course, but using the opportunity to circumnavigate Iceland in his ship, confirming that it was indeed an island. He landed in the north at Skjálfandi Bay and built a house on the shore, in the exact spot where you'll now find the town of Húsavík (House Bay). He stayed for a winter before sailing back to Sweden.

After Garðar, things really started to heat up. Flóki Vilgerðarson was the first to purposefully set out to Iceland, famously sailing with three ravens as a part of his crew to help him find Iceland. The first two ravens were no help – only flying up and landing back on the ship. But the third took off to the west, and Flóki and his crew followed it all the way to the southern shores of the Westfjords, coming ashore at a place now called Flókalundur. There he set up a camp, but after that just about everything went wrong. Flóki and his crew were so enamoured with the great fishing on offer in Breiðafjörður that they forgot to harvest hay for their livestock, which all died. Then he had to watch one of his best friends drift away on the ocean, never to return after the fishing boat broke loose from its mooring. To top it all off, the crew suffered through a frightfully cold spring. He was losing all enthusiasm for his adventure as he scaled a nearby mountain. From the top, he spied the next fjord overfilled with icebergs. It was the final straw. He dubbed the country Ísland (Iceland) and promptly sailed back to Norway in a huff.

Settlement

The first permanent settler in Iceland was Ingólfur Arnarson, who arrived in the year 874, marking the beginning of the Settlement

Age. He and those to follow were mostly from Norway – powerful chieftains and their families who had fallen out of favour with the Norwegian king, choosing instead to start a new life in Iceland. In just 50 years, around 30,000 people settled in Iceland, snatching up most of the coast and interior and divvying it up between friends and family. Then, in 930, the chieftains of these independent farms came together on the plains of Þingvellir (*see* p. 160) and established the Alþing, a nationwide parliament to help govern the country. Every midsummer from then on, people travelled from across the county to Þingvellir for what turned into the social event of the year, where big business deals were struck, weddings were announced and punishment for lawbreakers was meted out.

The Middle Ages

Iceland adopted Christianity in the year 1000, bringing an age of peace and prosperity to the country. But soon after, six families gained control of much of Iceland through their wealth and political machinations. The King of Norway began to play these families off one another as they looked to expand their power in Iceland, and soon, it was an all-out civil war. The result was Iceland falling under the rule of the Norwegian king after a period of violent battles. Not long after, Norway fell under the control of the Danish Crown, which scooped up Iceland as well as an added bonus.

From 1397 to 1944, Iceland remained a part of the Kingdom of Denmark. In 1602, a stringent trade monopoly was enforced on Iceland by the Danes, granting exclusive trading rights to select Danish merchants. This monopoly made these merchants very wealthy while significantly hindering Iceland's economic progress, isolating the small island nation from the rest of Europe during a

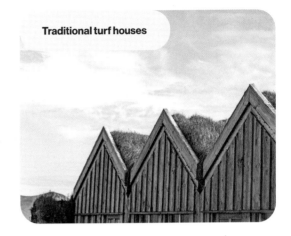

Traditional turf houses

ICELANDIC CULINARY PECULIARITIES

From fermented shark to pickled ram's testicles, the traditional food in Iceland isn't for the faint of heart. In the early days of settlement, the Vikings had to contend with the elements, without the comforts you'll find today. Food sources were scarce, and to survive the harsh winters, things had to be pickled, cured, dried, smoked over dung and fermented.

By far, fermented shark, or *hákarl*, is the most important traditional food in Iceland. Eating the meat of a Greenland shark without fermenting it is highly poisonous – and our thoughts go out to the first Vikings who found that out back in the day.

period of profound cultural transformation on the continent, thanks to the scientific revolution and the Enlightenment. While the rest of Europe thrived, Iceland suffered, and the Danish trade monopoly brought about privations, not helped at all by a series of natural disasters that fast-tracked widespread starvation on the island. After the plague ravaged Iceland some 40 years after Europe, the Danes finally decided to loosen trade restrictions, and from 1786, Icelanders were legally allowed to trade more broadly, bringing opportunity and increased chances for wealth.

Independence

During the 19th century, revolutions raged across Europe, sparking a significant change in politics in the region, and the Industrial Revolution changed the way societies functioned. This massive upheaval also led to a revival of a national consciousness in Iceland. Danish-educated Icelandic intellectuals began writing and publishing essays in a Danish journal called *Fjölnir*, which quickly became a demand for complete independence from Denmark. It was partially granted – Iceland received a constitution and limited home rule in 1874.

Then came the World Wars. While Europe suffered under consecutive conflicts that drained their resources, Iceland could export plenty in World War I, thanks to Denmark's neutrality. Then, in 1940, Denmark was swiftly occupied by Nazi forces in just a few hours. Soon after, the British arrived to occupy Iceland, thanks to its strategic location, which caused unemployment to disappear overnight. Icelanders across the country were employed to provide the British troops with food, shelter, and entertainment, until 1941 when the American military replaced the British. Suddenly, things were booming, and the US military set about greatly improving Iceland's infrastructure, building roads and airports and helping the standard of living catch up with the rest of Europe. By this point, years had gone by without any word from occupied Denmark, so Icelanders met and voted to end Danish rule. They sent a missive to the Danes and received a congratulations in reply. Iceland found itself an independent country for the first time since the 14th century.

Geography

Iceland's geography is its biggest attraction. Situated in the far north Atlantic Ocean, the island nation sits just south of the Arctic Circle, straddling the continental divide between the North American and Eurasian plates. This unique location and the fact that it's also situated on top of a hot spot in the Earth's core are the reasons Iceland is a treasure trove of natural wonder and geological spectacle.

Glaciers & Volcanoes

At the heart of Iceland's geography are its volcanoes. The country boasts over 130 active and dormant volcanic mountains, many of which lie underneath the highland glaciers. It's this combination of 'fire and ice' that gives Iceland's landscape all its drama, with eruptions behind fresh lava fields, craters, black-sand beaches and basalt cliffs, while the slow shifting of its glaciers carves out the deep fjords, valleys and lagoons. Millions of years ago, the same processes happened to the rest of the world; in Iceland, it's happening right now.

Icelandic horses roam the green landscape

Rivers & Waterfalls

Draining out of the highland glaciers are dozens of powerful glacial rivers that have carved out the country's deep canyons over time. Glacial floods caused by eruptions under the ice have also added their strength to these canyons, one of the reasons why Iceland has so many spectacular and powerful waterfalls. The other reason is thanks to the central highland plateau, a convenient ledge for rivers to launch themselves off as they spill down into the lowlands, draining out to the sea.

Geothermal Power

Iceland's volcanic zones also give rise to an abundance of geothermal power. This presents itself in different ways; it might be a natural hot spring in the middle of nowhere, offering a convenient place for a soak. Or a Mars-like landscape with belching mud pots, simmering blue pools and sulphurous fumaroles spewing out steam from below. Or it could be an oasis of unique colours in an otherwise barren landscape, where the geothermal power has caused minerals to react and create a unique landscape.

Flora & Fauna

Despite the harsh climate, Iceland has a surprising amount of unique flora and fauna. The country's flora is an abundance of sub-Arctic species, including famous types of moss usually clinging to lava fields or precipitous cliffs. The spring thaw brings an explosion of wildflowers and lupine fields and signals the imminent arrival of millions of seabirds, including the famous Atlantic puffin. The seabirds all find comfort in the rugged cliffs that ring the country, while ducks, swans and several species unique to Iceland take to the lakes and ponds scattered across the island. The longer daylight hours also make the deep fjords an attractive place for whales, and if you're lucky and head to the more remote corners of the country, you may even spy an arctic fox slinking about – Iceland's only native land mammal.

Mud pools at Hverir
Geothermal Area

EXPLAINING ICELAND'S RENEWABLE ENERGY

It's no secret that Iceland has an abundance of renewable energy. The country has long known the secrets to tapping into its volcanic roots, piping the naturally hot water found underground into 90 per cent of homes and businesses around the country. Generating electricity in Iceland is also 100 per cent renewable, although geothermal sources only account for roughly 25 per cent of this power. The other 75 per cent comes from hydropower, with power plants harnessing the massive amounts of meltwater rushing off the country's glaciers.

With all the country's electricity coming from renewable sources, it is no surprise that Icelanders have a carefree attitude when it comes to leaving lights and radiators on inside their homes. Geothermal energy also powers greenhouses like Friðheimar, ensuring the local food ecosystem is as environmentally friendly as possible.

But how does Iceland harness its geothermal energy? It starts with drilling a hole down to the large reservoirs of water that lie underneath the country. Heated naturally, thanks to the volcanic hot spot underneath Iceland, water vapour is extracted up through the drill holes to the surface. Then, it's separated into liquid water and steam. The steam is run through turbines, producing electricity for homes and businesses across the country.

Climate & Weather

Thanks to warm waters flowing from the Caribbean, up through the Atlantic and past the coast of Iceland, the country is saved from the freezing weather that this longitude implies. Iceland's dramatic weather is in part caused by this warm current as it collides with colder Arctic currents, creating new fronts and pressure systems that can swiftly push across the country in a matter of hours. This, alongside its geographical location and the confluence of Arctic and Atlantic air masses, all contribute to the volatile weather conditions in Iceland. It means rain, sleet, snow, strong gusts of wind, impenetrable fog and, outside of summer, howling blizzards – sometimes all in one day. But when the sun does appear (and it often does!), the country resembles an absolute paradise on Earth.

For many, summer is the obvious time to travel to Iceland, when the weather is at its calmest. But Iceland's weather is also an attraction. The sheer power of a storm, whipping winds and sideways rain are memories that remain fresh in the mind for far longer than the days of relative calm and warmth. Be prepared for strong gusts of wind unlike anything you've felt, and rapidly changing conditions that can bring snow one minute and sunshine the next. For more information about staying safe during Iceland's symphony of elements, see p. xxi.

Culture

Aside from all the astounding nature, the other big pull of Iceland is its unique culture. There's no way around it – Icelanders are simply cool, in every sense of the word. Just as Iceland's geology plays with a sense of time like no other destination, there's also a timeless quality to Icelanders. Strong-minded, independent and resilient, this tight-knit community knows how to face any challenges thrown their way. With a clear and direct connection to their ancestors, whose tales of struggle and resilience have been passed down through generations, Icelanders have a stronger bond with their history than many other cultures. This instils in them a profound sense of continuity and permanence.

Icelanders are also a creative bunch, and even those who don't work in a creative field often have a creative hobby. Again, this can perhaps be attributed to their culture of self-reliance, forced to entertain themselves during those long, dark winters, when storms howled outside and they had many an hour to fill. Today, that has translated into a budding music scene and a workforce that is adaptive and open to any changes that might be able to help them.

The more modern Icelandic culture is pleasantly underpinned with a strong undercurrent of Nordic mythology, folk tales and legends. Every Icelandic landscape seems to have a superstition attached to it, from sea stacks said to be trolls turned to stone to all the legends surrounding the Huldufólk, also referred to as the Icelandic elves. Given the harsh living conditions faced by the first settlers and the wild landscapes covered in all kinds of weather, it's easy to see how they began to see trolls, giants and other fantastical creatures in the landscape.

Finally, due to growing up around the unpredictable nature of their home country, you'll find most Icelanders are adaptable and upbeat even in the most dire of circumstances. The country's unofficial motto – *þetta reddast* – translates to 'it will all work out okay in the end', and in Iceland, that's usually true.

STEREOTYPES

The biggest stereotype about Iceland is that all Icelanders believe in elves. But there is a distinction to make here. The study most people quote doesn't show that over 50 per cent of the population believes in elves. Rather, it states that over 50 per cent of the population wouldn't completely discount the idea that elves could exist – an important distinction. In all seriousness, Icelanders are modern, up-to-date people. For more on the Huldufólk, *see* p. 189.

Top **A curious local**
Bottom **Strolling through Reykjavík**

TRAVEL INFORMATION

Getting Around Iceland

The best way to get around Iceland if you're not on an organised tour is with your own rental vehicle. Public bus routes are improving, but all the wild nature you want to see and explore is between the destinations these buses service. It would be strange to find a bus that drops you off in the middle of nowhere beside a raging waterfall. A car or campervan is best.

Driving in Iceland is also quite different to most places, but it's always an adventure. A single-lane highway encircles the country, known as Route 1 or the ring road. Taking you past most of the major highlights, it's a ready-made itinerary for your trip. However, this also means that most people who visit Iceland – over two million yearly – are also looking to do a loop of the ring road. You'll find the best bits when you venture off it.

Holidays & Opening Hours

The biggest holiday to note is Icelandic National Day (17 June) – otherwise, Christmas and Easter are also important holiday seasons.

Opening hours for general stores are from 9am until around 6pm or 7pm. On Saturdays, opening hours are slightly shorter, while on Sundays, many shops have reduced hours or are closed entirely.

Museums and tourist attractions are usually open between 10am and 5pm, but it goes without saying to check beforehand. Iceland's nature is open 24/7.

Basic Etiquette

Hot Spring & Swimming Pool Etiquette

One of the biggest surprises that catches visitors to Iceland off-guard is the etiquette involved in using local swimming pools and hot springs. In Iceland, it's required to completely nude up and shower before you hop in some hot water, giving yourself a good scrubbing with soap first. This is because Iceland's geothermal waters contain high levels of minerals and bacteria that can be harmful when combined with the bacteria on our skin. Showering removes most of this before hopping in the water, ensuring the water stays clean for everybody's use. For more information, *see* p. 6.

Tipping

Tipping is not required in Iceland since everyone makes a decent wage (Iceland has the highest average wage in Europe). Although, like in most places nowadays, you can round up in restaurants if you wish or tip a tour guide if they have provided an experience well above your expectations. It's not expected at all, but always appreciated.

How to Travel Responsibly in Iceland

Iceland's popularity has soared in the past decade, with over two million tourists visiting each year. With these numbers threatening to overwhelm natural attractions, responsible travel is more crucial than ever.

Iceland's unique ecosystems are extremely fragile, and the short summer season makes any damage more lasting. Always respect the rules in place: stick to marked paths to avoid causing lasting damage, never drive off-road and respect road closures – they are in place for your safety and the preservation of the environment.

Be aware of hot springs etiquette

Consider travelling outside the high season of July and August. Most visitors come during these months for favourable weather, but spreading tourism throughout the year can help reduce the impact on popular sites and provide a more serene experience. Spring and autumn offer beautiful landscapes, fewer crowds and a more intimate connection with Iceland's natural beauty.

Venture beyond the most visited attractions. The Westfjords is Iceland's least-visited region, yet it boasts some of the country's most spectacular scenery. Similarly, the Eastfjords are often overlooked due to the typical travel routes around the ring road. Slowing down and exploring these lesser-known areas can provide a richer, more sustainable travel experience.

For a truly memorable adventure, consider long-distance hiking. National park ranger Elias Arnarson recommends carving out time for these hikes, which allow you to immerse yourself in Iceland's landscapes without the crowds. While you might not see every famous landmark, you will return home with unique and unforgettable stories.

By travelling responsibly and thoughtfully, you can help preserve Iceland's pristine

THE ICELANDIC PLEDGE

The 'Icelandic Pledge' is a set of guidelines to help educate visitors and protect the country's environment.

* I pledge to be a responsible tourist.

* When I explore new places, I will leave them as I found them.

* I will take photos to die for, without dying for them.

* I will follow the road into the unknown, but never venture off the road.

* I will only park where I am supposed to.

* When I sleep out under the stars, I'll stay within a campsite.

* And when nature calls, I won't answer the call on nature.

* I will be prepared for all weathers, all possibilities and all adventures.

For more information about responsible tourism, head to the chapter on sustainable initiatives in Iceland (see p. 77).

environments for future generations while enjoying a more rewarding and respectful journey. For responsible travel ideas, *see* p. 77.

Icelandic Language

The Icelandic language is one of the culture's most unique traits, remaining mostly unchanged for over 1000 years. Due to the country's isolation, Icelandic didn't evolve alongside other Scandinavian languages. Today, it's the closest thing to Old Norse – Icelanders today can still read their texts from the early days of settlement.

Despite a strong command of English across the country, it goes without saying that a willingness to try out some local phrases will go a long way with locals. Here are some common phrases and their pronunciations to impress the Icelanders you run into, even though they'll quickly switch over to English.

– **Hello:** Halló (ha-loh)
– **Goodbye:** Bless (bles)
– **Thank you:** Takk (tahk)
– **Yes:** Já (yow)
– **No:** Nei (nay)
– **Excuse me:** Afsakið (av-sa-kith)
– **May I have?:** má ég fá? (mau yeh fow)
– **I don't understand:** Ég skil ekki (yeh skil eh-ki)
– **Do you speak English?**: Talarðu ensku? (ta-lar-thu en-sku)
– **Where is the bathroom?:** Hvar er klósettið? (kvar er klo-set-id)
– **Help!:** Hjálp! (hya-ulp)
– **I'm lost:** Ég er týnd/ur (yeh er tind/ur) – use týnd if you're a woman, týndur if you're a man
– **How much does this cost?:** Hvað kostar þetta? (kvath ko-star thet-ta)
– **I am a vegetarian:** Ég er grænmetisæta (yeh aer graen-metis-eye-tah)

Currency & Money

Iceland has its own currency, the Icelandic krona (ISK), with a longstanding reputation for fluctuations and instability. Still, those fluctuations never really affect the price of

Möðrudalskirkja church

things when you're in the country; expect to fork over a small fortune for everything from petrol to groceries.

Iceland is expensive for two reasons. The first is that, as an island, it must import most things. And with such a small market, the number of things it imports is far less than other European countries, which means Iceland doesn't get quite as good a deal from the suppliers. The other reason is its remote location; Icelanders figured out long ago that they could charge whatever they wanted for things. If you're not going to buy it here, where else can you get it?

Cash is basically nonexistent in Icelandic society, and even at the most remote campsites or cafes, the owner will whip out a brand-new machine to accept payment. One of the few exceptions is coin-operated showers at campsites. These still exist in places, so having some coins on you is handy. But again, usually at these campsites, you can pay by card, and the warden can add a little extra and give you the coins they have generally retrieved from the showers.

Safety

Iceland is one of the safest countries in the world, topping the list of countries on the Global Peace Index for over a decade and counting. Petty crimes are almost nonexistent, as are violent crimes, although recently there have been warnings of pickpocketing at the major sights on the south coast, so keep your wits about you. Solo travellers, particularly solo female travellers, rave about their experience in Iceland. Of course, just like any other destination, it pays to be cautious, and with increased tourism comes increased petty crime.

WEATHER WARNINGS

When things get hairy in Iceland, the IMO has a simple and easy-to-understand warning system.

* **Green:** Normal weather conditions.

* **Yellow:** This weather warning means some 'moderate' weather conditions exist. These can range from strong winds and snow to rising temperatures, causing increased glacial runoff and swelling rivers to potentially break their banks. Yellow weather warnings also might mean travel isn't recommended, and you best bunk down wherever you may be.

* **Orange:** An orange weather alert is reserved for even stronger winds and powerful storms, such as gale-force winds and heavy rain, wind gusts that might sweep a car off the road or heavy snow and white-out conditions.

* **Red:** A red weather alert is for a state of emergency when storms, volcanic eruptions or earthquakes pose a risk to lives and property.

Rest assured that if you're travelling in the country and bad weather hits, you'll hear about it from tour guides, hotel staff, restaurant workers and everyone else. Weather is the biggest conversation topic in Iceland.

Safety in Nature

Talking about safety in Iceland also means talking about the danger present in the natural landscapes. Icelanders live alongside the risk of volcanic eruptions, avalanches, glacial floods, earthquakes and fierce winds throughout the year. The weather can also present conditions unfamiliar to many travellers; a sunny day can rapidly turn to rain, sleet or a blizzard, and before you know it, a once-pleasant outing has turned life-threatening. That's why it's important to keep tabs on the weather and log your travel plans with Safe Travel (safetravel.is). This ensures the Icelandic Search & Rescue Team (*see* p. 83) knows how many people are in an area if there's an adverse weather or natural event.

Luckily, the Icelandic Meteorological Office (IMO) is pretty handy when predicting the most dangerous natural events – volcanic eruptions and glacial floods – which means you shouldn't have to worry about getting caught unawares. Alerts for adverse weather events are put out through the website and their app, warning you of anything you need to know about.

Finally, if you plan extensive hiking, you'll need to be prepared. The right gear is essential – a waterproof jacket, pants and shoes, warm gloves and a hat – and for more serious endeavours, a GPS, hiking poles and a good sense of navigation.

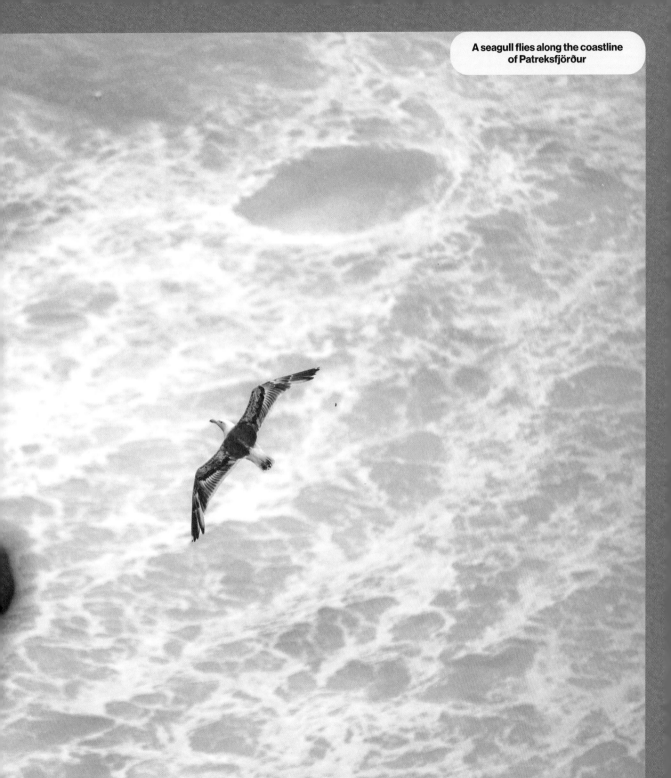

A seagull flies along the coastline of Patreksfjörður

Falljökull Glacier, Vatnajökull
National Park

BEST OF ICELAND

ICELAND'S NATURAL SHOW-STOPPERS

The Golden Circle

The Golden Circle is the perfect introduction to Iceland. Usually completed in an easy day trip from Reykjavík, this well-trodden tourist route takes in three spectacular natural sights. The first is Þingvellir National Park, a place of historic importance where the first settlers gathered to form Iceland's parliament, called the Alþing.

Next is Geysir, the erupting geyser from which all others are named (although Geysir no longer erupts, the name has stuck for the entire area – luckily, its little sister 'Strokkur' erupts every five minutes or so).

Finally, there's the thundering waterfall Gullfoss (see p. 51), sitting at the edge of the Highlands a multi-tiered behemoth of a cascade with glaciers glinting in the background.

Vatnajökull National Park

Europe's largest national park is a playground for adventurers, encompassing the glacier Vatnajökull and the vast swathes of earth that have been shaped by it through successive eruptions and glacial floods. This national park's canyons, valleys, rivers, and lava fields offer a look at the elemental power that has sculpted Iceland into the country you see today. At the same time, the glacier is popular for its glacier hikes and, in winter, the ice caves underneath.

We dip into the park with a ranger (see p. 34) and talk about its main territories in-depth (see p. 37).

Jökulsárlón Glacier Lagoon & Diamond Beach

The south-east corner of Iceland is home to two of the country's most spectacular and famous attractions: the Jökulsárlón Glacier Lagoon and Diamond Beach.

Jökulsárlón is an expansive lagoon that emerged as the glacier Vatnajökull retreated, leaving behind a vast body of water crowded with icebergs as they fall off the retreating glacier tongue making its way back up into the mountains. Those icebergs are then shaped by the winds and currents, and eventually they are pulled out to sea through a small inlet. But instead of floating away, the strong ocean tides wash the icebergs back onto a black-sand beach, where they're left to melt slowly, warping into a natural sculpture gallery known as 'Diamond Beach'.

Lake Mývatn

East of Akureyri on the ring road, you'll come across the steaming area of Mývatn, which is filled with lakes and wetlands and is a hot spot for birdlife in the summer. Sitting directly atop the Mid-Atlantic Ridge, it's also one of the best places in the country to witness the power at work just below the surface.

Loop around Lake Mývatn itself, and you'll discover things like the vast Dimmuborgir lava field, the towering Hverfjall Volcano, steaming mud pots, belching fumaroles and pseudo craters.

The area is also home to the popular hot spring Mývatn Nature Baths, North Iceland's answer to the Blue Lagoon, filled with gloriously warm water and boasting views over the volcanic landscapes.

Landmannalaugar

The colourful rhyolite mountains of Landmannalaugar are among the country's most famous landscapes. These vibrant peaks were sculpted by a series of volcanic eruptions – a testament to Iceland's fiery heart.

Located in the southern Highlands the hiking here is considered the best in the country, offering a nonstop tableau of jaw-dropping views and geological wonder. It's also the beginning of the famous Laugavegur Trail (*see* p. 38), Iceland's best multiday hiking trail that leads you south through the volcanic landscapes to the oasis of Þórsmörk (*see* p. 48), a nature reserve nestled between three glaciers.

Opposite **Vatnajökull Glacier hike**
Top **An impressive ice shard at Jökulsárlón Glacier**
Bottom **Inside an ice cave in Vatnajökull National Park**

The Northern Lights & Midnight Sun

Iceland's natural beauties aren't purely bound to the country itself but also play out in the skies above. Its position just south of the Arctic Circle means that in summer, Iceland enjoys long hours of daylight, with the summer solstice in June offering a chance to see the sun grazing the horizon at midnight before gently lifting itself back into the sky. It's a magical time in the country, as are the months in the lead-up and wind-down. The long hours of daylight also mean that you can stay out exploring long into the evening and the wee hours of the morning, your adventures lit permanently by a beautiful and fuzzy golden hour.

Of course, the trade-off for all this beautiful light in the summer is Iceland's short winter days. At the peak of winter, you can expect only around four hours of daylight before darkness returns. But with this darkness comes a very sought-after experience: witnessing the northern lights. Thanks to its position in the far North Atlantic, the skies above Iceland are ideal for catching sight of the dancing green curtains of light, a chemical reaction occurring as particles from the sun collide with the Earth's magnetic field. Watching the waves of green ripple across a dark sky is an amazing experience you won't soon forget.

Opposite **Aurora Borealis,
the Northern Lights**

Top **Trekking along
Falljökull Glacier**

Glaciers & Ice Caves

Iceland's glaciers cover about 11 per cent of the country's land mass, offering a chance to explore the icy world. The four largest are Vatnajökull, Hofsjökull, Langjökull and Mýrdalsjökull, but there are countless others found atop mountains in the furthest reaches of the Highlands. From far away and up close, the ice is beautiful, shifting between hues of white and blue all the way to black, showcasing volcanic ash trapped by the ice after an eruption.

The best way to get acquainted with Iceland's ice is to join a glacier hike. The area around Skaftafell (*see* p. 37) in the south-east has been designated as the centre for glacier excursions. However, you can also find tours that lead up onto Eyjafjallajökull and Mýrdalsjökull in the south. These hiking tours start with a super jeep driving you to the glacier's edge (each year, the drive becomes longer as the glacier retreats) before you follow your guide up onto the ice, crunching around with crampons while the guide explains how glaciers are created and points out glacial tidbits like deep crevasses, natural arches and jagged ice walls.

As autumn brings cooler weather to Iceland, ice caves begin to form underneath the glaciers, thanks to the summer meltwater flowing under the ice slowly freezing over. Come winter, these rivers freeze up completely, leaving behind ice caves stable enough for tours to venture inside. This is, without a doubt, one of the best experiences you can have in Iceland, glimpsing the frozen world underneath Europe's largest glacier.

Hot Springs & Swimming Pools

It's hard to overstate just how important swimming pools are to Icelandic culture. Blessed with abundant geothermal hot water bubbling up to the surface, Iceland has harnessed this power and diverted it into hundreds of swimming pools and more than a few luxurious hot springs across the country. Then there are what Icelanders call *náttúrulaugar* (natural pools), where the hot water has collected by itself somewhere in nature, ideal spots to enjoy a dip while immersing yourself in the Icelandic landscape, whether the hot spring is nestled in some hills, by the base of a glacier or the bed of a river. We've rounded up our five favourite natural hot springs on p. 44.

You can find a local swimming pool in every town around the country, each with one or sometimes two larger pools, as well as several hot tubs with temperatures ranging between 36°C and 44°C (97°F and 111°F). Sitting in one of the various hot tubs somehow erases the superficial boundaries we place between each other. Whether you're a politician or a plumber, in the water you're just two people, and it's at swimming pools that Icelanders discuss the daily news and gossip. For travellers, it offers a moment to connect with the locals or even other travellers, trading Iceland tips and tricks, discussing the weather and road conditions and helping each other out with any worthy additions to itineraries. Some pools will also have steam rooms, Finnish-style saunas and ice baths.

SWIMMING POOL ETIQUETTE

Visiting swimming pools in Iceland comes with its own specific etiquette.

First and foremost, you must always remove your shoes before entering the changing rooms. Once inside, find a locker, change into your swimwear and grab your towel.

Then, there's the small matter of stripping down naked in the communal showers and giving yourself a thorough scrubbing. Swimming pools in Iceland use limited chlorine, so this is a necessary step before hopping in the water. There are racks to store your towel (you'll leave it here until coming back in after your swim), soap dispensers and posters on the wall illustrating all the spots you'll need to wash. And if you don't? Expect the Icelanders to tell you off.

After your shower, put your swimwear back on and rush outside into the cold and windy weather to dive into either the swimming pool or a hot tub.

Some pools, mainly those in Reykjavík, now offer gender-neutral changing areas. If you're unsure, ask the front desk staff for guidance. If you're trans, you have the right to choose which changing room you use.

Seljavallalaug, a geothermal swimming pool

REYKJAVÍK – THE CAPITAL

Reykjavík is Iceland's compact capital, basically a large town with the vibes of a much larger cosmopolitan city. A constant flow of visitors from across the world helps give the downtown area an infectious atmosphere, and you'll find countless restaurants and bars, unique boutique stores, museums and kitsch souvenir shops to keep you busy. With a few days at the beginning or end of your Iceland trip, here's how to make the most of your time in Reykjavík.

Day 1

Morning Start your first morning in Reykjavík by heading over to Deig Bakery for coffee, fresh doughnuts and New York–style bagels. The location puts you right next to the old harbour, a nice spot for a brisk stroll along the waterfront to admire the ships in the dock (keep your eyes peeled for the Icelandic Coast Guard ship or any luxury yachts). Eventually, you'll reach Harpa (*see* p. 198), the glittering ultra-modern

Sun Voyager sculpture

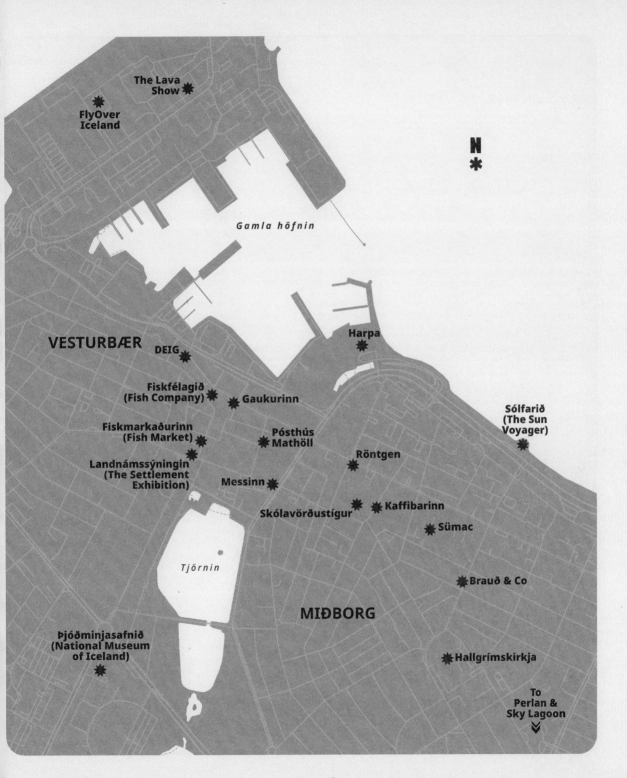

The Lava Show

FlyOver
Iceland

N

Gamla höfnin

VESTURBÆR

Harpa

DEIG

Fiskfélagið
(Fish Company)

Gaukurinn

Sólfarið
(The Sun
Voyager)

Fiskmarkaðurinn
(Fish Market)

Pósthús
Mathöll

Röntgen

Landnámssýningin
(The Settlement
Exhibition)

Messinn

Skólavörðustígur

Kaffibarinn

Sümac

Tjörnin

Brauð & Co

MIÐBORG

Þjóðminjasafnið
(National Museum
of Iceland)

Hallgrímskirkja

To
Perlan &
Sky Lagoon

concert hall perched on the water's edge, and the Sun Voyager sculpture further along, representing the early Vikings' journey sailing west from Norway to Iceland. Then, head up the hill toward Iceland's most famous landmark, the Hallgrímskirkja church. Duck inside and up the tower to drink in the views over the city.

Afternoon For lunch, stroll toward the centre of town along Skólavörðustígur, now more commonly known as the 'rainbow street', thanks to its painted rainbow on the pavement. Then, make your way to Messinn for fresh fish plucked from the ocean that morning, served in a hot pan alongside potatoes, a healthy dollop of sauce and a crisp salad. After eating, dedicate the rest of your afternoon to one of the capital's many museums: visit the National Museum for a broad overview of Icelandic history, or head for the Settlement Exhibition to see the remains of a Viking longhouse.

Top **The skyline of Reykjavík**
Bottom **Overhead view of the city**
Opposite **Colourful Skólavörðustígur Street**

Evening Whether it's summer or winter, spending an evening at the Sky Lagoon is a fantastic idea. The late opening hours mean that come summer, the soft glow of the midnight sun illuminates the infinity pool, with views across the bay to a peninsula where the Icelandic president lives at Bessastaðir. In winter, things are darker and more mysterious, with winds whipping the steam away into the inky sky, where, hopefully, the northern lights shine above.

Day 2

Morning On the morning of your second day, start off with coffee and some cinnamon scrolls from the bakery Brauð & Co, inside a graffitied building in downtown Reykjavík. Then, it's time to experience some of the capital's more engaging exhibits. The Lava Show (*see p. 130*) is the only place in the world, outside of a volcanic eruption, where you can see lava up close. At the same time, FlyOver Iceland offers an immersive ride over the country's spectacular landscapes. Or you could try the Wonders of Perlan exhibit, where interactive exhibits on all of Iceland's geological wonders help you understand the powers at play in the country. You'll also find an artificial replica of an ice cave and fantastic views over the city from the observation deck.

Afternoon For lunch, try the Pósthús Food Hall, a collection of different restaurants occupying the former downtown Icelandic Post Office. After you've eaten, enjoy another stroll through the downtown area, stopping by the national parliament and church on Austurvöllur Sq. A short walk from here is the city's pond, Tjörnin, where you can admire a huge topographical map of Iceland on display inside the City Hall. Afterwards, there are plenty of great shops along Laugavegur and Skólavörðustígur for souvenirs, be it Icelandic design or anything else.

Evening For dinner, the Fish Company offers some of the best seafood in town. If you'd rather try Icelandic fusion, Sumac offers a blend of Icelandic ingredients and Eastern Mediterranean dishes, or there's the Fish Market, which creates fantastic sushi and other Japanese-inspired dishes on the only robata grill in Iceland. After dinner, it's time to sample that famous Icelandic nightlife. On weeknights, bars are open until 1am, while from Thursday to Saturday, they stay open until the wee hours. Hunt down some happy hours before heading to the staples of the scene: Röntgen for an atmospheric, lounge-style bar, Gaukurinn for live comedy, music and drag shows, or Kaffibarinn for late-night DJs.

WEST ICELAND & THE KJÖLUR ROUTE

Forgo the ring road for this tour through historic West Iceland, cutting through the historic Kjölur Route in the western Highlands with a 4WD.

DAY 1
The Golden Circle

The country's most popular day trip is called the Golden Circle, the name given over to the region north-east of Reykjavík where a trio of major sights offer a first look at Iceland's incredible nature. There's Þingvellir National Park (see p. 160), and then the Haukadalur geothermal area, where the geyser called Strokkur erupts every three to five minutes in a clap of water and steam. Then, there's the thundering Gullfoss waterfall, one of Iceland's largest, a multi-tiered cascade crashing down a valley etched into the earth at the edge of the Highlands.

DAY 2
Kerlingarfjöll & Hveravellir

From the top of the Golden Circle, strike out along F35, the historic route between north and south Iceland the Vikings used on their way to meet at Þingvellir. Aim for Kerlingarfjöll (see p. 147), a mountainous region of steaming geothermal valleys and hot springs, perfect for hiking. After you've finished there, continue to the geothermal oasis of Hveravellir further north along the route, with more boiling hot springs and one suitable for swimming right by the river. A guesthouse here offers a remote stay in the desolate landscape.

A small mountain hut in Hveravellir
Opposite **Kerlingarfjöll Mountains**

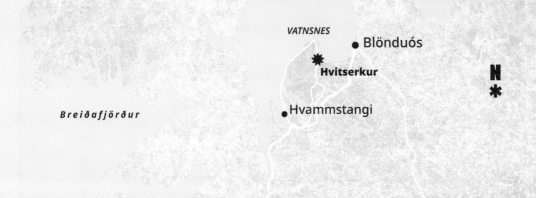

VATNSNES

● Blönduós

✴ **Hvitserkur**

Breiðafjörður

● **Hvammstangi**

N ✳

SNÆFELLSNES

Hveravellir ✴

Hofsjökull

Viðgelmir ⋀

≫ *Hraunfossar*

Langjökull

Borgarnes ●

Kerlingarfjöll ✴

Þingvellir National Park ✴

≫ *Gullfoss*

REYKJAVÍK ◎

This page and opposite top **Hiking in the Kerlingarfjöll Mountains**

Opposite bottom **Steps leading into Víðgelmir lava cave, near Húsafell**

DAY 3
North-west Iceland

After finishing the F35 route, you'll emerge in north-west Iceland, an underrated region often overlooked by ring road travellers. Venture up onto the Vatnsnes Peninsula, where Hvítserkur rock resembles an elephant rising out of the black sand of the beach. Continue bumping around the peninsula to see seals on the western edge, and then spend some time in the lovely village of Hvammstangi, a quiet and peaceful spot to spend the evening. If you're feeling adventurous, you could instead tackle the Beast of the East on a whitewater rafting trip (*see* p. 144), with tours departing just south of the town of Varmahlíð.

DAY 4
Into the West

From Hvammstangi, follow the ring road back toward Reykjavík, veering off into the knot of rivers and roads north-west of Borgarnes. Here, you can stop at Hraunfossar, a wide waterfall spilling out over cliffs from underneath a lava field, and the lava cave Víðgelmir, one of the largest in the world carved out by a lava river. Finish up at Hotel Húsafell, where you can take an optional tour into a nearby canyon to visit their secretive Canyon Baths hot spring or simply enjoy the local swimming pool.

THE SNÆFELLSNES PENINSULA

The long arm of the Snæfellsnes Peninsula claws its way out into the ocean from the western coast, jutting out above Reykjavík like the gnarled finger of a giant. Many travellers overlook this stretch of countryside in a rush to whip around the ring road, but the peninsula is often described as 'Iceland in miniature', providing a crash course in the varied Icelandic landscapes you'll find around the country. There are lava fields and bubbling hot springs, black-sand beaches and epic sea cliffs, volcanic craters and lava tubes, and culminates in the icy fingers of the Snæfellsjökull glacier. On a clear day, you can see Reykjavík, and vice versa; the white cone of Snæfellsjökull can often be seen from Reykjavík, the brooding volcano serving as a reminder to the city folk of just who is in charge here.

DAY 1
The Southern Shore

Set out north from Reykjavík, veering off the ring road just after the town of Borgarnes. As you near the beginning of the peninsula, you'll spy the mountain range that cuts down the middle, separating the southern shore and the north coast. Between the road and the coast to the west rises a large crater called Eldborg, presenting a great opportunity to stretch your legs on a 90-minute return walk. Then, the southern shore takes you past huge swathes of farmland, where you'll see horses in paddocks and sheep with their lambs in spring.

Stop by Búðakirkja to see Iceland's only black church framed by the mountains and glacier behind, and then clamber your way through the Rauðfeldsgjá gorge as it cuts into the mountains separating the north from south. Then, the villages of Arnarstapi and Hellnar are separated by about half an hour's worth of coastline perfect for walking, with twisted basalt arches, sea caves and thousands of nesting birds.

DAY 2
Snæfellsjökull National Park & the North Shore

Start early on your second day and venture into the Snæfellsjökull National Park (see p. 42), a place wrought by eruptions over the ages that have left the landscape littered with vast, lava fields and craters. There are desolate beaches both black and gold, huge craters scarred red from volcanic activity and lava fields laden with moss for exploring on foot. Along the coastline, lava has spilled into the ocean and created twisted cliffs, covered with nesting seabirds come summer.

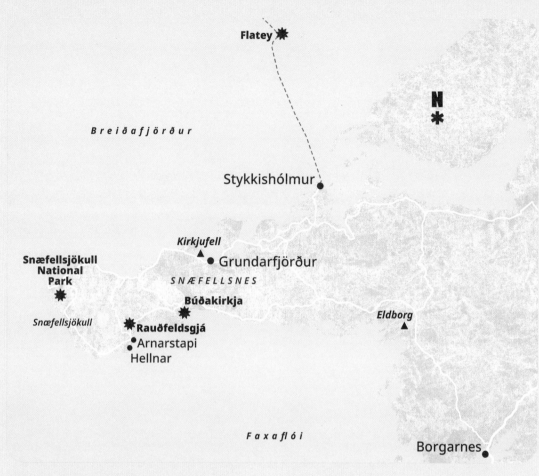

Flatey

B r e i ð a f j ö r ð u r

N
*

Stykkishólmur

Kirkjufell
▲
Snæfellsjökull
National
Park
● Grundarfjörður
S N Æ F E L L S N E S

Búðakirkja

Eldborg
▲

Snæfellsjökull
Rauðfeldsgjá
●Arnarstapi
Hellnar

F a x a f l ó i

Borgarnes

When you've finished inside the national park, the northern shore of Snæfellsnes is home to a clutch of small fishing villages that still do a brisk trade, thanks to their location on Breiðafjörður. This vast fjord separates the peninsula from the Westfjords. Grundarfjörður is most popular for its stunning surroundings and proximity to Kirkjufell, the country's most photographed mountain. Stykkishólmur is also a nice port town, dotted with historic Danish trading houses and home to the ferry that takes you to Flatey Island (*see* p. 207) as it crosses Breiðafjörður to land on the southern shore of the Westfjords.

A sea arch on the coast of Arnarstapi

NORTH ICELAND & THE ARCTIC COAST WAY

A newly launched driving route tempts the adventurous with 900km (560 miles) of untouched northern coastline, where black-pebbled beaches are dotted with driftwood, strong winds do battle with basalt cliffs and snow-kissed peaks and profound solitude is to be found. The Arctic Coast Way traces the intricate coastline of seven peninsulas – each boasting geological wonders, legends and wildlife – culminating in the quaint hamlet of Bakkafjörður.

DAY 1
Vatnsnes & Skagaströnd Peninsulas

Beginning in the village of Hvammstangi, the route careens first around the Vatnsnes Peninsula, famous for its seals on the west coast. Once you've rounded the tip and are on the eastern side, detour down to Hvítserkur, a giant rock that resembles an elephant rising from a black-sand beach. After a brief stint on the ring road, the route veers up toward the little-visited village of Skagaströnd, where the Museum of Prophecies details local stories of witchcraft. The coast above is littered with basalt cliffs made from ancient eruptions, while on the north-east corner are the impressive Ketubjörg cliffs, where a waterfall spills down into the fierce North Atlantic.

Siglufjörður town centre, North Iceland
Opposite **Turf houses in Skagafjörður**

ICELAND *SEA*

Raufarhöfn
LANGANES

Kópasker
Þistilfjörður

Öxarfjörður

Þórshöfn

Siglufjörður
Bakkaflói

Eyjafjörður

Ketubjörg
Skjálfandi

Húsavík

Bakkafjörður

SKAGI

Skagafjörður

TRÖLLASKAGI

Skagaströnd

Sauðárkrókur

VATNSNES

Akureyri

Goðafoss

Mývatn

Hvitserkur

Hvammstangi

N

DAY 2
Skagafjörður, Tröllaskagi & Akureyri

Skagafjörður is home to some of Iceland's most storied landscapes; it was here that the deadliest battle during the Viking Age took place, causing the Norwegian King to take control of the island. Learn about it, and the Viking clans who battled for control, through virtual reality at the museum 1238: Battle of Iceland. Other than that, the countryside is known for its beautiful farmland and horses. The next peninsula over is Tröllaskagi, a hotbed of adventure sports, thanks to its jagged peaks perfect for remote heliskiing. At the tip is Siglufjörður, a town once one of Iceland's biggest ports due to the bountiful herring found just off the coast. It became a ghost town once they were fished out but has since reclaimed some of its former glory with increased tourism.

DAY 3
Lake Mývatn, Húsavík & Jökulsárgljúfur

Akureyri sits pretty on one side of Iceland's longest fjord, Eyjafjörður. The modest city is home to a fantastic botanical garden as well as some interesting art museums and good restaurants. But the volcanic nature on show at nearby Lake Mývatn is hard to beat (with a stop at Goðafoss first of course), including pseudo craters, twisted lava fields and a giant strato volcano. Up north, Húsavík acts as the capital of whale watching in Iceland.

DAY 4
Melrakkaslétta & Langanes

A remote and little-visited area, these two final peninsulas offer incredibly stark landscapes. The relatively flat interior gives way to the coast, filled with driftwood and the cries of thousands of gulls. Points of interest

Outside the Herring Era Museum, Siglufjörður

Top left **Fish hung up to dry in Hvammstangi**

Top right **People walking around the steaming geothermal area of Hverir in the Lake Mývatn area**

Bottom left **Overlooking the small village of Hjalteyri, on the fjord Eyjafjörður**

include the epic cliffs around the beaches at both Kópasker and Raufarhöfn, the two specks of villages that anchor either end of the peninsula and the Arctic Henge, a spin on Stone Henge. Then, the harbour of Þórshöfn acts as the gateway into the Langanes Peninsula, an abandoned area of the country home to epic sea cliffs, a former port and small village left to erode in the elements and the remains of a radar station operated by the US military during World War II.

THE WESTFJORDS

Huge fjords, silent mountains and a strong sense of tradition amongst the locals – this is the Westfjords. Far away from everything else, this is Iceland's least-visited region and one of the most beautiful.

DAY 1
From Reykjavík to Látrabjarg

The start of the Westfjords Way isn't anywhere in particular. From Reykjavík, things begin to feel different as soon as you veer off the ring road after the town of Borgarnes and pass Búðardalur. Fewer cars are on the road, more sheep are roaming the fields and quiet, abandoned farmhouses stand on distant hills. From Búðardalur, in about 45km (28 miles),

you'll cross a long bridge built over a fjord and enter the Westfjords proper.

This southern stretch of Westfjords is our favourite. Rough, gravel roads are a wonderful introduction to the region, dipping in and out of the fjords. Beautiful beaches mark this part of the region along the coast and the islands of Breiðafjörður. Hidden beneath the road just before the hotel at Flókalundur is one of the best hot springs in the country called Hellulaug (*see* p. 44). From here, the scenery unfolds into something spectacular, crossing into Patreksfjörður. Take the bumpy roads to both Látrabjarg (*see* p. 68), Iceland's westernmost point, and the golden sands of Rauðisandur.

Driving through the Wesfjords

DAY 2
The Central Westfjords

After a night in Patreksfjörður, take the scenic route along the coast. Dirt tracks lead out onto the peninsulas, where you can discover stunning beaches and views, while the little towns are havens for waffles (see p. 101) and good food. Choose between the hot pots outside Tálknafjörður (Pollurinn) or Bíldudalur (Reykjafjarðarlaug) for a soak – or visit both – before making your way to Dynjandi waterfall, the crowing jewel of the Westfjords. There are more quaint villages to explore further north: In Þingeyri you can rent bikes to cycle around the peninsula, Flateyri has the oldest store in Iceland selling Icelandic books in English, while out the other end of Suðureyri is a fine example of a turf house, built by locals. Ísafjörður is the region's capital, with restaurants, cafes and some beautiful hikes in the surrounding area.

A restored Viking hovel outside of Suðureyri

Opposite top **Golden sands of Rauðisandur Beach**

Opposite bottom left **An abandoned barn in Fossfjörður**

Opposite bottom right **The historic fishing village of Bolungarvík**

DAY 3
The Northern Westfjords

A tunnel connects Ísafjörður with the more northerly town of Bolungarvík, a historic fishing village where sailors have plied the ocean since the settlement era. Here, a huge viewpoint on top of the mountains offers unfettered views of Hornstrandir (*see* p. 71), one of the last true wildernesses remaining in Europe. Then, the road delves eastward further into the long fjord, dipping in and out and offering waterfalls in valleys, quiet stops and the chance to spot seals lazing on the shores. At Reykjanes, an Olympic-sized swimming pool tempts you for a dip in hot water, while behind the hotel you can find Saltverk (*see* p. 94), where salt is made using the geothermal power on the peninsula.

For further explorations in the region, consider venturing up the Strandir Coast, with a one-way road into one of the most isolated areas of Iceland, where driftwood washes up on the jagged, spindly coast and its bays. At the far end, a surprise awaits: Krossneslaug, a swimming pool that feels as if it's at the end of the earth.

THE SOUTH COAST

The most popular regions in Iceland are worthy of the hype. The south coast is the country's most well-trodden region, but visiting outside of July and August means fewer crowds, while still giving you plenty of daylight to explore. In this region, farmers have stubbornly carved out land in the shadows of the glaciers, and over the years, they have had to contend with eruptions and huge glacial floods that have given the countryside all its drama.

DAY 1
The Golden Circle

Rather than drive directly towards the coast, spend a day first looping through the Golden Circle north-east of Reykjavík. This area gives you plenty of bang for your buck when it comes to Iceland's incredible scenery, and the roads naturally flow back down towards the ring road anyway when you're ready to whisk yourself down to the south coast for your second day on the road. In this area of countryside wedged between the capital and the Highlands, you'll find Þingvellir National Park (see p. 160), of course, and then the Geysir, from which all others are named (although it's Strokkur that erupts, not Geysir – confusing, we know). Finally, at the edge of the Highlands, you'll find the powerful waterfall Gullfoss, and you can cap off your day with a dip in the Secret Lagoon, a historic hot spring in the small town of Flúðir.

DAY 2
The South Coast

Nip down to the ring road and you'll find yourself drawing closer to the south coast. You'll know you've arrived when you spy Seljalandsfoss cascading off the highland shelf – not long after that is Skógafoss, a sheet of white spray that crashes down between mossy-green cliffs. Further along the ring road, closer to the country's southernmost point, lies the Dyrhólaey Peninsula, a huge outcrop and sea arch where you can see puffins and gawk at the thin ribbons of black sand stretching in either direction. One of those beaches is Reynisfjara, the country's famous black-sand beach, where basalt columns rise from the sand and twist into intricate sea caves.

DAY 3
Vatnajökull National Park

Driving east from Vík along Route 1 brings you to the expansive Skeiðarársandur, a huge swathe of black sand and glacial wash dumped here by previous eruptions from underneath the glacier, Vatnajökull (*see* p. 34). When they do occur, it's mostly this vast plain of sand that suffers through glacial floods. Continue driving until you reach the Jökulsárlón Glacier Lagoon, one of the star attractions of the ring road but nowadays more popular, thanks to Diamond Beach just across the road, where chunks of glacier wash up on a stretch of black sand and slowly melt into fascinating natural sculptures. Continue to Höfn and you'll quickly get an idea of just how vast the glacier is – rough dirt tracks branch off the ring road and bump towards the ice, leading to secretive glacier tongues and lagoons in an area that's still underrated by most.

DAY 4
Return to Reykjavík

It's a long drive from Höfn back to Reykjavík, but you can visit some of the sights you missed along the way. Stop by Skaftafell for the hiking trails, and then the twisting Fjaðrárgljúfur Canyon west of Kirkjubæjarklaustur. Between the waterfalls Skógafoss and Seljalandsfoss you can find Seljavallalaug, a historic swimming pool where locals once learned to swim, nestled at the base of the glacier Eyjafjallajökull. Then, within a couple hours you can be back in Reykjavík, sipping a beer at happy hour downtown.

Fjaðrárgljúfur, also known as the 'feather river canyon'

"It's a place that feels contemplative and ethereal"

NATURE

TIME & SILENCE

⊙ VATNAJÖKULL NATIONAL PARK

Vatnajökull National Park is a behemoth, covering a huge swathe of the eastern side of Iceland – approximately 13 per cent of the country's land mass. This is the largest national park in Europe, and few of the continent's natural paradises can boast such grandeur. Beyond the easily accessible entry points on the ring road lies another realm entirely. Most of the park's territory is within the Highlands region, an inhospitable and remote area of Iceland that only opens for the short summer every year. Here, travellers find themselves mostly alone in a primordial world, where the glacial rivers, windswept deserts of black sand, volcanic craters and jagged canyons are stark, unforgiving and utterly enthralling.

Elías Arnar is a national park ranger who spends his summers stationed inside the national park, guiding those adventurous tourists who make the most of the short summer season to visit its most remote area. For the past few years he has been stationed at the Dreki Mountain Hut, just outside of the Askja volcanic caldera north of the glacier.

'For me, the special thing about this national park is the silence. Not a day goes by when I don't think to myself – wow, look at that incredible view – but there's also something so special about the absolute silence you can experience that is hard to put into words. It's like you're in your own world, surrounded by endless views of mountains, of ash desert or glacial ice.'

Elías's job isn't just to help visitors with what to see and do in the park but also to educate them about its protection. 'Most people don't know why in Iceland we're so strict when it comes to off-road driving and staying on the paths. It's because, whereas in other places the flora might have a period of six months to grow and recover, in Iceland, it's only a couple of months. If someone ventures off the path or drives off the road, they're creating marks in the terrain that are going to be there for a long, long time.'

Askja itself is becoming more popular, but it still lies beyond the reach of regular vehicles. To get here, you'll need a 4WD and the guts to ford a handful of rushing glacial rivers – not for the faint of heart. Once you've arrived, you'll find yourself in an active volcanic area, a brooding place where you're not even a blip on the radar of the power that shifts underneath. But that's a part of the appeal as well.

'One of the most memorable experiences I had was a day when some people came back from the Viti crater and mentioned that they had seen some smoke rising from the crater. We really didn't know why there would be smoke other than some volcanic activity starting, so we drove to check it out. I was on edge the whole way,' Elías says.

'There were definite signs of an impending eruption, but in the end it all died down and nothing happened. But the feelings I had on that day really made an impression on

me – it was such a strong reminder that we're completely at the mercy of nature out here. It's beautiful, but also unforgiving.'

Askja and other destinations in the Highlands, such as Lakagígar, Snæfell and Nýidalur, offer a look at the extremes of Vatnajökull National Park. There are also easier places to access the park, like Skaftafell in the south and Jökulsárgljúfur in the north, both short detours off the ring road and wildly popular. But for Elías, the best way to visit Vatnajökull National Park is to give it the time it deserves. 'If you can carve out a long period of time to do a multiday hike in the Highlands, then it's truly the best way to experience the park. On foot, it's a different world. Hiking through the ashen desert to reach the fringes of the glacier and watching the landscape slowly change from black sand to jagged ice is truly an unreal way to immerse yourself in the country's nature.'

Vatnajökull National Park is Iceland at its most raw and powerful. There are no inhabitants, limited services, and a visual feast of natural landscapes to gawk at, all while completely at Mother Nature's mercy. And a nearly endless amount of silence – you just need to set aside the time to truly appreciate one of the last remaining wildernesses in Europe.

Top **Svartifoss Waterfall**
Bottom **Svínafellsjökull Glacier**

Skaftafell

Cradled in the southern valleys of the glacier Vatnajökull, Skaftafell remains the easiest place to access the national park. Here, you can experience all the living and breathing aspects of the largest glacier in Europe; the area is a wonderland of mountains and ice, black sand and glacial water.

Much of Skaftafell is protected by a bowl-shaped set of hills, which is why it's said the weather is better here than just outside. There are glacier tongues that spill down through the mountain passes, and on approach to the park, you'll pass through the huge glacial outwash plain called Skeiðarársandur, where glacial floods have scarred the landscape with boulders and in past eruptions, washed away the bridges that you'll be crossing.

Because it's time that has created all that is exciting in Skaftafell, time is what is really needed here to appreciate the sheer magnitude of the nature on show. Highlights include Svartifoss Waterfall, a picture-perfect cascade rushing out over a set of hexagonal basalt cliffs, and views over the Skaftafellsjökull Glacier Tongue, which continues to recede at an alarming rate. The mountain Kristínartindar presents a perfect challenge for longer day hikes, rewarding hikers with uninterrupted views over the Vatnajökull glacier. Or to the west of the main trails, the glacial valley of Morsárdalur offers a seven-hour return hike to a remote glacier tongue and some of the area's most remote and gargantuan landscapes.

Jökulsárgljúfur

The northernmost territory of Vatnajökull National Park is called Jökulsárgljúfur, the name given to the deep canyon etched into the landscape by the Jökulsá á Fjöllum River. Separated from the national park's main boundaries, this is a place of strange and twisted landscapes created over thousands of years by eruptions and immense glacial floods.

At the very edge of the Highlands, the river drops into a series of powerful waterfalls, the largest of these being Dettifoss. At its strongest, this is the most powerful waterfall in all of Europe, with around 500 cubic metres (130,000 gallons) of water rushing over the edge every second. To put it into perspective, that could fill an Olympic-sized swimming pool (about 2.5 million litres) in roughly five seconds. The rush of this waterfall reverberates through the surrounding landscape, a desolate place of giant boulders carried here by floods from the glacier.

Further north along the canyon, you'll see evidence of volcanic activity. At Hljóðaklettar, you can see the cores of ancient volcanoes, left behind after floods swept all that was loose away into the lower basin. And then there's Ásbyrgi Canyon, a giant horseshoe-shaped imprint in the earth that was said to have been created in just a few days, blasted out via the floods. Considering the canyon walls here reach up to 100m (330ft) high, it's hard to comprehend such force. Today, it's home to a visitor's centre and some excellent hiking trails that trace the canyon's rim.

LEGENDS ON ICELAND'S LAUGAVEGUR TRAIL – A HIKE THROUGH ICELANDIC GEOLOGY

⊙ SOUTHERN HIGHLANDS

This famous multiday trek through Iceland's Southern Highlands is one that every serious hiker will have on their to-do list. To walk through the primitive terrain stretching from Landmannalaugar to Þórsmörk is to undergo a crash course in Icelandic geology, taking you back in time, with each layer of lava, rock and moss marking an epoch of days gone by.

DAY 1
Landmannalaugar to Hrafntinnusker: Rhyolite & Lava Fields

One of the enduring pictures travellers will have of Iceland is that of the rhyolite mountains at Landmannalaugar. Streaks of red, orange and yellow course through this pretty set of hills, created through volcanic eruptions where magma rich in minerals like iron, sulphur and other trace elements exploded onto the landscape, cooling into the colours you see today. Contrasting with the rhyolite mountains is a spectral lava field, made up of jagged obsidian formed from magma that seeped out of the nearby volcano around the year 1477. These are the first steps you take on the Laugavegur Trail,

through the lava field – said to be the haunt of trolls and Huldufólk (Icelandic elves) – and into the colourful mountains beyond, hiding steaming geothermal valleys and patches of wildflowers until you reach the mountain hut at Hrafntinnusker.

DAY 2
Hrafntinnusker to Álftavatn: Mountains & Distant Glaciers

From the mountain hut at Hrafntinnusker, the hike continues up into the mountains – the second day is a day of peaks and valleys, ridges, cliffs and canyons. On a clear day, you can catch your first glimpse of the glaciers to the south, punctuating the horizon and providing a contrast to the earthy hues of the mountains you're trekking. Descending the mountain chains you'll enter valleys dotted with vibrant moss and wildflowers, with streams trickling down from the surrounding peaks. Eventually, the blue lake of Álftavatn comes into view, sitting in a basin surrounded by jagged hills with the mountain hut on its tranquil shores.

The peaks around Álftavatn

DAY 3
Álftavatn to Emstrur: Volcanic Desert & Desolate Flood Plains

From Álftavatn, the hike brings you steadily closer to the volcanoes; soon, you'll leave the rolling hills and meadows near the lake behind and enter a volcanic desert of ash, black sand and rocks left behind from eruptions in days past. Those eruptions from beneath the glaciers also released raging *jökulhlaup* – or glacial floods – sending huge amounts of meltwater through the glacial rivers that course through the black sand. You'll have to cross several of those rivers today, surrounded by towering cliffs and rock formations that give this part of the Laugavegur a true prehistoric atmosphere. Then, the trail descends into more lush valleys, leading you to the mountain hut at Emstrur, perched on the foothills leading up to the fringes of the glacier Mýrdalsjökull.

DAY 4
Emstrur to Þórsmörk: Glacial Rivers & Volcanoes

There are more rivers and streams to cross on the fourth day of the trail, the final stretch where the landscape morphs from desolate volcanic desert into lush green canyons and rushing rivers. Þórsmörk (*see* p. 48) is an area of hidden valleys beneath a chain of volcanic mountains and glaciers, where hundreds of glacial rivers pour down the mountainsides and combine into a braided swathe of interlocking rivers that course through the black sand of the valley. It's an area of immense beauty, where you can see the black pumice of ash and sand, moss-green mountains and ashen grey basalt cliffs, steely blue rivers and shining white glaciers. Low-lying birch forests are protected from the winds and give the area its name – Þórsmörk means 'Thor's Wood' in English, and legend has it that the thunder-wielding deity himself created the area with a lightning-swift swing of his hammer, Mjölnir.

JOURNEY TO THE CENTRE OF THE EARTH

⊙ SNÆFELLSJÖKULL NATIONAL PARK

The smallest of Iceland's three national parks, Snæfellsjökull National Park covers the very tip of the Snæfellsnes Peninsula, the long arm of the country that arches out above Reykjavík. Centred on the icy summit of the glacier Snæfellsjökull, it's home to twisted lava fields laden with moss, black and golden beaches flanked by warped cliffs of basalt, secretive lava caves and explosive craters.

For many, this is a place that holds a strange power. French novelist Jules Verne wrote about Snæfellsjökull over 150 years ago in his famous novel *Journey to the Centre of the Earth*, despite never having seen the ice cap. In the novel, the volcano acts as the entrance to the centre of the earth, with his protagonists venturing into the lava tubes to a secret world underneath. The glacier cropped up again in the media in the '90s, when a British man declared that aliens had told him they would be landing on the glacier on 5 November. Over 500 people gathered there that blustery winter's evening, including a news crew from CNN, but the aliens didn't come. Still, there's no denying that this is a special place.

The volcano last erupted over 1800 years ago and is one of Iceland's 32 active volcanic systems. In contrast to the raw and primordial volcanic landscapes of Vatnajökull National Park, Snæfellsjökull is far more tranquil. Sloping down from the icy summit of the glacier, you'll find huge lava fields that stretch all the way to the coast, in places having spilled into the sea to create incredible sea stacks. There are huge craters but also quiet beaches and easy trails that meander through the rubble of eruptions past – cliffs, craters and basalt. It's a place that feels contemplative and ethereal rather than explosive and raw. To fall under its spell yourself, check out our itinerary of the Snæfellsnes Peninsula (*see* p. 16).

A HOT POT ODYSSEY – THE BEST HOT SPRINGS IN ICELAND

⊙ AROUND ICELAND

While Iceland might be eternally embraced by chilly winds and frequent rains, it is also a land blessed with an abundance of naturally occurring hot springs. Icelanders are rightly proud of their bountiful hot water, and they learned long ago how to use this to their advantage; there are more swimming pools per capita in Iceland than anywhere else, and swimming culture is a big part of Icelandic culture (*see* p. 208). Beyond the local pools and luxurious hot springs (like the Blue Lagoon), you can also find more natural hot springs across the country, where hot water bubbles up from underground to collect in rock pools and shallow ponds and stream down rivers, ideal for a soak in the middle of nature. Add some rain, wind or snow, and you have a full-blown elemental experience that's hard to beat.

Hellulaug, Westfjords

Those who make the journey out to the Westfjords are rewarded with an abundance of hot springs to choose from wherever they visit. One is a highlight: Hellulaug. Located on the southern shores of the fjords, a short drive away from where the ferry docks after crossing Breiðafjörður (*see* p. 207), this natural rock pool is hidden below cliffs by the coast. Overlooking Vatnsfjörður, a protected nature reserve, it's a wonderful place to soak up the silence, watching the sky and water change colour, with plenty of birdlife going to and fro.

Grettislaug, North Iceland

Next on our hot spring hot list is Grettislaug, located on a remote peninsula in northern Iceland. From the town of Sauðárkrókur, a bumpy and gravelly road leads you out along the eastern side of the peninsula, ending up at a farm where you'll find the Grettislaug hot spring. It's one of the nicest hot springs in the country, built into an area of black sandy rocks and overlooking the distant island called Drangey, whose dramatic basalt cliffs jut up from the waters in the middle of the fjord, flocked by crying gulls and rocked by wind and waves. It's a dramatic sight to see on a stormy day – now imagine making the swim to shore from the island because that's exactly what the Viking outlaw Grettir the Strong did before recovering in the hot spring.

Laugarvellir, Eastern Highlands

In the area near Kárahnjúkar Dam at the edge of the eastern Highlands, you'll find one of Iceland's coolest hot springs: Laugarvellir.

What makes this one so special is that it's a waterfall of hot water – that's right, hot water cascading over a cliff like a natural shower and collecting in the rock pool below. Upon first sight it seems as if it's the ploy of some crafty tourism business, but no, this is entirely natural (and free of charge). This is an excellent spot to enjoy remote landscapes, 4WD adventure and the reward of soaking in hot water.

Reykjadalur River, South Iceland

One of the more well-known hot springs in Iceland is the Reykjadalur River, in the geothermal mountains that rise behind the town of Hveragerði on Route 1 heading south. It's a popular spot nowadays, but it is still worth the hour-long trek to reach the part of the river where hot and cold water combine to create the perfect temperature for bathing. Along the way, you'll pass steaming fumaroles, glowing blue pools and gloopy mud pots that gurgle and burp. To avoid the major crowds, visit late at night in the summer (around midnight is perfect), when the skies never fully darken.

Hveravellir, Western Highlands

Another fantastic hot pot makes for a nice stop for those traversing F32 in the Highlands, commonly referred to as the Kjölur Route (*see* p. 54). A historic place that served as the main highway for the early Vikings travelling from the north to meet the other clans at Þingvellir, Hveravellir must be one of the oldest rest stops in the country. It's a geothermal hot spot, home to brooding, boiling pools of water, scorched patches of earth and wafts of sulphurous steam. But there's also a lovely large pool by the river where the hot water has been collected, ideal for a dip in hot water.

Top **Reykjadalur is also known as 'steam valley'**

Bottom **Taking a dip in the Reykjadalur River**

Top left **Grímsey Island – the 'edge of the earth'**

Top right **Lighthouse on the coast**

Bottom **Grímsey Island's harbour**

BEYOND THE ARCTIC CIRCLE

◉ **GRÍMSEY ISLAND**

If you find the coast of Northern Iceland windswept and isolated (*see* Arctic Coast Way, p. 18), you'll be amazed at the feelings that envelop you if you visit Grímsey Island. This is Iceland's remotest inhabited island, and besides a few resolute islanders and millions of seabirds, there's nothing here but steely basalt rocks, sharp winds and frothy waves crashing into the shore on all sides.

Being so remote, Grímsey is hit with the full force of Iceland's brutal weather systems. In the 'calm' months of summer, it's pretty much always blustery, and rain, sleet, hail and snow are commonplace; add in the crashing waves made angry by the winds whipping down from the north, and the island often feels as if it's in the middle of a tempest. But there are moments of silence and calm, too, made beautiful in summer by the midnight sun hovering over the distant horizon, and in winter when the northern lights streak across the sky in deep greens, blues and reds.

Visiting Grímsey feels as if you're at the edge of the earth – the next stop is the North Pole. Frequent flights from Akureyri and ferries from Dalvík are scheduled, but whether they leave or not is a different story. This is a place where the weather can change rapidly, and one look at a storm descending on Grímsey and you'll understand why a pilot might not feel like trying to land a plane there. But the unpredictability of arriving and departing imbues the island with its unique charm. And as for exactly where the Arctic Circle crosses Grímsey, head to the northern end of the island where a huge concrete sphere tracks the shifting boundary of the Arctic Circle, which is inching further north due to a slow wobble in Earth's rotational axis.

VOLCANO TRAILS
◎ ÞÓRSMÖRK NATURE RESERVE

Bumping over the black sand scarred by glacial rivers, I spy out of the corner of my eye a white object immersed in the river. It's a car of course – a small 4WD that had decided to ignore all advice from Icelandic car rentals and try to tackle the swift-flowing rivers coursing through the valley leading to Þórsmörk Nature Reserve.

My bus driver stops before crossing the river, calling someone on his phone to come fish them out. Then he simply continues to drive, fording the same river with ease in his bus equipped with giant wheels. As we drive past the car, he rolls down his window.

'Someone will be along shortly to help!' he casually calls to the panicked-looking tourists stuck in the river. We continue our drive into Þórsmörk, fording several more glacial rivers along the way, and stopping for a break near a glacier tongue.

'These rivers are some of the hardest in Iceland to cross,' he muses to me as we admire the glacier above us, clinging to the jagged cliffs. After a short rest, our driver waves us back onto the bus, and we continue into the nature reserve proper.

Nestled in an area north of the glacier Eyjafjallajökull, Þórsmörk translates to 'Thor's Wood'. It's a name that sparks an idea

of a Nordic paradise, and that's what you get – verdant birch forests, towering waterfalls rushing down intricate basalt canyons and braided rivers interlocking through a bed of black sand. In this labyrinth of chasms and canyons, all the colours of Iceland are on show.

I set up in the dorms at the Volcano Huts, only a few other beds occupied inside. I immediately set out to explore, spending a long day wandering deep into the valleys of the nature reserve. My chosen trail at first meanders through a birch forest to a nearby mountain hut, set at the base of the valley. From here, I venture further into the valley, making my way deeper into the reserve along the side of the cliffs, the steely grey and black basalt slowly elevating me above the black sand below.

For hours I hike, at one point emerging at a viewpoint towards the end of the valley. A remote mountain hut further south catches my attention, dwarfed by the sheer mountains and the glacier above. There's some movement on the mountain, and I realise that there are a few hikers coming down from the elevated mountain pass, Fimmvörðuháls. It's a gruelling day trek that links Þórsmörk with Skógafoss waterfall on the south coast, leading you between the two glaciers and past where the 2010 Eyjafjallajökull eruption wreaked havoc on air traffic across Europe. Other than those specks of hikers I'm alone on the trails.

Back at the Volcano Huts that afternoon, I recover at an outdoor table and bench, watching as hikers arrive and collapse in a heap after having just finished the final stage of the Laugavegur Trail. Beers flow freely in the restaurant, and I quiz people on their experience tackling Iceland's most famous long-distance trek (see p. 38). Soon, the bus arrives, and they pile in, drunk, happy, and on their way back to Reykjavík.

The next day, more of the same – extensive hikes into the valleys, views over the glaciers and black sand and steely glacial rivers winding their way through the bedrock. The sun is shining, and the glaciers are impossibly white and still. With such calm weather, I feel as if I've discovered the real paradise in Iceland. Thor was onto something here.

Later that evening, I'm bumping my way back to the ring road on the bus. There's no car as we cross the river – someone must have come along and towed them out of the water. Þórsmörk remains one of Iceland's most untouched natural paradises, only accessible by those who tread carefully. In other words, don't drive – just catch the bus instead.

🌐 volcanotrails.com

Mountains overlooking the Krossá River

Top **Photographing Dynjandi Waterfall**

Bottom **Gullfoss Waterfall**

CHASING WATERFALLS

⊙ AROUND ICELAND

It's no secret that Iceland has plenty of waterfalls to keep water enthusiasts enamoured with the country for several lifetimes. Thundering down from precipitous highland cliffs, etched basalt valleys and spilling off glaciers, stopping to admire the power of water in Iceland is a highlight of any trip. Below, we've rounded up the absolute best of the best.

Gullfoss

Gullfoss Waterfall is the culmination of the Golden Circle (see p. 12), the most popular day trip from Reykjavík. It's an impressive end to the day, tumbling down the Hvítá River, which originates from Langjökull Glacier in the Western Highlands. It's called Gullfoss (Golden Falls) for the rainbows that are often created when the sun appears to light up the spray drifting up from the bottom of the canyon.

Skógafoss

Darling of the south coast, Skógafoss is a perfect sheet of white water tumbling off the Highland shelf. Nestled between moss-laden cliffs, it's a hot spot for tourists. But leave the crowds behind by following the trail up past the waterfall (the beginnings of the Fimmvörðuháls Pass into Þórsmörk) where you can discover even more waterfalls. Or visit nearby Kvernufoss, hidden at the end of a short valley to the east.

Dynjandi

The crowing jewel of the Westfjords is Dynjandi, a thundering waterfall that cascades over several huge steps etched into the cliffs. The result is mesmerising, as the waterfall gets wider at the bottom before spilling down towards the fjord over a series of further falls, each with a viewing platform. Located in a remote valley in the Westfjords, this is a highlight of a journey through this little-visited region.

Dettifoss

The country's most powerful waterfall is Dettifoss, nestled in the huge landscapes of Jökulsárgljúfur Canyon (see p. 37). Charging off the cliffs and plummeting down 30m (100ft) to the bottom, it's a small glimpse at the true power of Iceland's glaciers – this represents but a fraction of the force of glacial floods sent hurtling down rivers from underneath the country's glaciers.

Goðafoss

North Iceland's other gem is Goðafoss. This postcard-perfect waterfall is said to be the place where an Icelandic chieftain threw his Pagan Idols into the water after the country adopted Christianity in the year 1000. Hence the name Goðafoss, or 'Waterfall of the Gods'. For many, it's a favourite in the country, with great viewpoints letting you get up close to the surprisingly powerful waterfall.

Skógafoss Waterfall

THE KJÖLUR ROUTE

◉ **HIGHLAND PLATEAU**

The ancient Kjölur Route is a winding road that connects north and south Iceland. As one of the major routes that the Vikings took to travel between the regions, it has a storied past. The Icelandic Sagas recount tales of armies using the Kjölur Route to hurry from conflict to conflict, and thanks to its remote and unforgiving nature, it was also an ideal place for outlaws to hide out. Today, it's a designated F-road, requiring a 4WD vehicle to cross.

From the southern end, F35 begins after Gullfoss, the culmination of Iceland's popular Golden Circle (*see* p. 2). From here, the road climbs onto the Highland plateau, leading travellers through a pair of glaciers alongside massive lakes and a few outposts of civilisation. It's a spooky place, and despite it being one of the country's more trafficked F-roads, it still offers a good dose of isolation.

It also has its fair share of grisly tales. During the 18th century, it gained huge notoriety for its unforgiving nature due to two brothers. Having travelled to the south to purchase a new flock of sheep, the brothers found themselves in the unenviable position of having to return to their farm in the north using the Kjölur Route as winter closed in. Taking their chances, they started the journey, but after only a few days, their worst fears came true. A violent storm closed in around them, and temperatures plummeted. As they scrambled to keep their sheep in one place, they lost their way from the marked route, and eventually froze to death not far from the trail. When their remains were discovered, the Icelanders dubbed the spot Beinhóll (Bone Hill).

Today, driving the Kjölur Route provides an adventurous journey into the Highlands of Iceland, the desolate plateau marked only by two huge hot springs and geothermal areas.

ENTER ICELAND'S VOLCANIC HEART

⊙ THRÍHNÚKAGÍGUR LAVA CAVE

Iceland's volcanic systems are churning just below the country's surface, shifting, pulsing and surging, a labyrinthine network of molten rivers whose pressure carves out chambers in the darkness. And rarely does an opportunity present itself to delve deep into one of these magma caves – but there is one place you can, and it's the only place like it in the world: Thríhnúkagígur. Lava once oozed, sloshed and oscillated here, building and releasing pressure. In turn, the magma chamber was rocked by earthquakes and the tectonic plate rift. All that action spurred an eruption about 4500 years ago, but instead of the lava cooling afterwards in the chamber, it simply disappeared. Normally, this would cause the chamber to collapse in on itself (creating a caldera like that found in Askja, see p. 132), but that didn't happen either. Instead, the chamber was left empty but intact, and was discovered by Icelandic cave explorers in 1974.

It wasn't until two decades later that they started exploring the cave more deeply.

Delving inside, they spent several years venturing down into the darkness, dangling from ropes, headlamps shining in the immense, empty chamber. In 2010, National Geographic came to film inside, and the Icelanders needed to come up with a way to transport the camera equipment into the heart of the volcano. They decided on a modified window cleaning lift, like the ones you see clinging to the sides of skyscrapers. Today, this is what tours into the volcano use, whisking you down into one of the fiery hearts of Iceland for a look around.

The beauty of this place is found in the mineral deposits in the chamber wall, causing a kaleidoscope of earthy reds, oranges, yellows, greens and blues. The sheer magnitude of the space is also intimidating, to say the least – it's an unmatched look at the immense proportions and power at play beneath Iceland's surface.

Top **Signs mark potential danger on the Kjölur Route**

Opposite **Visitors can travel 120 metres (395 feet) into Thríhnúkagígur**

THE NEW VOLCANIC FIRES

◉ **REYKJANES PENINSULA**

The Reykjanes Peninsula in Iceland's south-west corner is one of the country's most interesting yet overlooked areas. There's far more here than just the airport and Blue Lagoon, with the region home to violent landscapes shaped by thousands of years of volcanic fallout. With ashen lava fields, wind-whipped mountain ridges and shifting black sands, many people think that the further you are from the international airport, the closer you are to Iceland's wilderness. But this is just about as far out as things get in Iceland, the entire landscape resembling what artists might depict as some distant planet.

In 2021, the Fagradalsfjall volcano erupted, spewing fresh lava onto the peninsula for the first time in around 800 years. It erupted again in 2022 and then again in 2023, causing volcanologists to theorise that the peninsula has entered a new period of heightened volcanic activity. This new period could last decades – even centuries – with earthquakes leading to eruptions across the peninsula.

That prediction came true at the end of 2023, when an eruption occurred in a parallel volcanic system, causing fissures to crack open along the Sundhnúkur crater row, sending lava creeping out towards both the Blue Lagoon and the Svartsengi Power Plant, which provides hot water to the entire peninsula. Since that first eruption, there have been three more from the same volcanic system, constantly threatening the infrastructure in the area, with lava even swallowing three houses on the edge of Grindavík, which had been evacuated after it was discovered magma was coursing into the ground beneath the town.

While Iceland is used to volcanic eruptions and can devise fantastic ways to divert lava from its infrastructure, during a period of extended volcanic activity, it's hard to say what will happen to the population centres around the peninsula's coast.

A small volcanic eruption
on the Reykjanes Peninsula

Top **River flowing through Katla Geopark**
Bottom **The glacial Katla Volcano**

A VENGEFUL SORCERESS

⊙ **KATLA VOLCANO**

The Katla Geopark is a vast swathe of land in South Iceland, marked by charging waterfalls, fertile farmland and huge black-sand beaches along the coast. One of Iceland's most destructive volcanoes, Katla, presides over it all as the creator of these landscapes.

Sitting underneath the Mýrdalsjökull ice cap, Katla has erupted on average once every 50 years. However, the last eruption was in 1918 – so it's long overdue. With the ice over 700m (2300ft) thick in some points above the volcano, eruptions might not even break the surface – but they do cause glacial floods to rush south toward the coast.

Katla is a popular girl's name in Iceland, and the legend surrounding the volcano is intriguing. Legend has it that Katla was a cruel and grumpy woman who worked as a housekeeper at Þykkvabæjarklaustur monastery on the south coast. It was rumoured that she owned a pair of pants that granted the wearer the ability to run unimaginably fast without tiring. However, no one was quite sure whether it was true or not.

Also local to the area was Barði, a shepherd who, one day at the end of the summer, needed to round up his missing sheep. An impending storm meant that he had to do it quickly, so he decided to find out if the rumours about Katla's magic breeches were true. Stealing into her home, he found the pants, took them and rounded up his sheep in record time. He returned the pants, but Katla knew that he had used them.

Flying into a fit of rage, she drowned Barði in a vat of whey. But as people continued to drink the whey over the course of the following weeks, she knew that one day his body would be discovered. Before it happened, she threw on her magic trousers and dashed towards the mountains, throwing herself into a large crack in the glacier Mýrdalsjökull. Since then, it has been said that the fiery and vicious sorceress has been behind the volcanic eruptions, many of which have had devastating results due to glacial floods.

UNTAPPED NATURE

◉ THE EASTFJORDS

On road trips around the country, the rhythms of driving distances and major sights usually mean that travellers skip through the Eastfjords in a day or two, zipping past to get to Vatnajökull glacier in the south-east or Lake Mývatn further north. That just leaves the area untouched for those who like to slow down and appreciate spectacular landscapes.

Lagarfljót Lake

Stretching south-west of Egilsstaðir, the largest town in the region, is the glacial lake called Lagarfljót. Legend has it that the steely waters of this lake are home to a sea monster like the Loch Ness Monster in Scotland. Farmers in the region have sighted the worm swimming in the waters over the years, but there was never any hard proof. To put the rumours to rest, the Icelandic Government announced a cash prize for anyone who could prove the monster exists. Then, in 2012, a local farmer caught the worm on video, cashing out the 500,000 ISK prize after his footage went viral.

Hengifoss Waterfall

On the western banks of Lagarfljót rises a steep mountain where the impressive Hengifoss waterfall is located. Shooting off a cliff and plunging down 128m (420ft), this is one of the country's tallest cascades. What makes it extra special, though, are the dramatic cliffs that flank the waterfall. These cliffs showcase distinct red clay and black basalt layers and offer one of the best visuals of volcanic eruptions and geological processes.

Seyðisfjörður

Tucked away at the end of a winding mountain pass east of Egilsstaðir, Seyðisfjörður enjoys arguably one of the finest settings in Iceland. Surrounded on both sides by towering peaks where waterfalls cascade down to the fjord, you'll easily be able to compare it to scenes from a fairy tale. In town, traditional Danish trading houses are painted bright colours and hug the base of the fjord, reflecting beautifully in the water when the weather is calm. The town pulsates with creative energy, and you'll find several art galleries and workshops to explore, if you can pull yourself away from the surroundings for long enough.

Stuðlagil features incredible basalt rock formations

Stórurð

Stórurð, also known as 'the Giant Boulders', is a stunning expanse of meadows and small pools, all framed by towering, jagged mountains. True to its name, the area is dotted with enormous boulders, seemingly left behind by retreating glaciers at the end of the last Ice Age. Or perhaps, as local legends might suggest, by trolls. Accessing this remote gem within the Dyrfjöll mountain range requires a challenging hike. The trek is approximately a 12km (7.5-mile) round trip from the nearest starting point and includes a few steep sections; a rewarding journey for adventurous hikers.

Stuðlagil Canyon

Located near the Jökuldalur Glacier Valley running down from Vatnajökull, Stuðlagil Canyon is one of the best places to get up close to basalt columns. The canyon shelters the 150km (93-mile) glacial river, Jökla, as it rushes north-east to drain out into the sea through a bed of black sand. Historically, the Jökla river was so treacherous that it split the Jökuldalur Valley in two, isolating farmers and communities on either side. To address this and to generate power for a nearby aluminium smelting plant in Reyðarfjörður, the Kárahnjúkar Dam was constructed. This lowered the water level of the river and revealed the hidden beauty of the basalt columns within.

"This might just be one of the best bird-watching places in Europe."

WILDLIFE

Top **Humpback whales are a highlight of Húsavík**
Bottom **Húsavík Whale Museum**

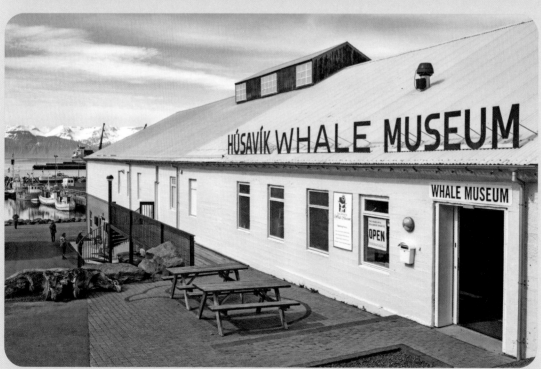

IN SEARCH OF GIANTS

⊙ HÚSAVÍK

In Iceland, there's always a chance you'll see a whale anytime you're near the water. From acrobatic humpbacks to pods of orcas to the reclusive blue whale, Iceland has found itself in the pleasant position of being a top spot for whales. Seen swimming off the coast and breaching in the fjords, people come to Iceland for the landscapes, only to be surprised that it's also a premier destination for spotting the world's largest animal.

Of all the locations in Iceland where you can see whales (pretty much anywhere), Húsavík in the far north has become a favourite haunt of the gentle giants. That has led to the University of Iceland setting up their Whale Research Centre in town, from where Dr Marianne Rasmussen takes charge of several long-term research projects.

'We always are working on a variety of projects at once. We have PhD candidates conducting their own research, as well as the main project of the Research Centre,' says Marianne. 'One of our major projects has been our photo-identification study, where we collect photographs of whales and add them to our ever-growing database.'

These identifying photographs (also called 'fingerprints') help researchers understand the migration paths of whales and the other whales they like to hang out with. Estimating things like age and total population is also possible, thanks to the huge photo set. 'This, in turn, helps us provide better information to shape policy that protects the whale populations in Iceland,' says Marianne.

Skjálfandi Bay is the ideal place to conduct such research, thanks to its combination of shallow and deep waters and abundance of marine life – an all-you-can-eat buffet for the whales. There are humpbacks, minke whales and even rare sightings of blue whales, who only come up for air every 20 minutes. All the stars aligned in this small bay in the north of Iceland, and several whale-watching outfits depart on tours multiple times per day in the summer. Húsavík has become known as the whale-watching capital of Iceland, beating both Reykjavík and nearby Akureyri.

The Research Centre gets most of its data by collaborating with the whale-watching tour companies. 'We send our research interns out on the tours, whose job it is to take photos of any whales that are sighted,' says Marianne. And the data flows in – throughout all the years whale-watching tours have been running, there has been a 98 per cent success rate.

'Even the public can help us with the research. If you take any photos, submit them to us and we'll add them into our database,' says Marianne. And if you see a blue whale? Count yourself lucky – they only show up on about 2 to 5 per cent of tours.

To submit your own photos of whales from Skjálfandi Bay, head to hvalasafn.is.

PUFFINS IN ICELAND

AROUND ICELAND

A big attraction of travelling to Iceland in the summer months is the chance to admire quirky Atlantic puffins. To see them up close, head to one of the following locations between April and August. For more on puffin rescue efforts, *see* p. 79.

Látrabjarg Cliffs, the Westfjords

Iceland's westernmost point is called Látrabjarg, a towering set of cliffs stretching along the southernmost peninsula of the Westfjords. Plunging over 400m (1300ft) into the seething ocean below, the location is a sight to behold, let alone when the cliff face is covered in thousands of puffins. This might just be one of the best bird-watching places in Europe.

Vestmannaeyjar, South Iceland

The archipelago of islands off Iceland's south coast is called Vestmannaeyjar, or the Westman Islands. Emerging from volcanic eruptions under the sea, these dramatic young land masses offer up jagged and sheer cliffs, twisting high into the air and providing puffins with ideal perches for their summer.

Borgarfjörður Eystri, the Eastfjords

In the far north of the Eastfjords, the remote town of Bakkagerði sits in a fjord called Borgarfjörður, designated with Eystri (East) to differentiate it from Borgarfjörður in the West. Here, on the far side of town, a small rocky cliff is a popular nesting spot for puffins, with a boardwalk taking you right through the middle for close-ups.

Dyrhólaey Peninsula, South Iceland

Dyrhólaey is a giant peninsula just west of Reynisfjara Beach and the town of Vík, a huge sea arch and mountainous area with a lighthouse on top. Paths trace their way along the twisted lava cliffs where you can see puffins winging their way between the ocean and the nests, bringing fish back for their chicks.

Flatey Island, Breiðafjörður

The only inhabited island out of the thousands located in Breiðafjörður, Flatey is also a place where you'll find puffins nesting in the summer. To get here, catch the ferry from Stykkishólmur on the Snæfellsnes Peninsula to the southern shores of the Westfjords at Brjánslækur. For more on Flatey, *see* p. 207.

A colony of puffins overlook
the south coast

Top **Arctic foxes are the patrolling locals of Hornstrandir**

Bottom **The pyramid-shaped peaks of Hornstrandir**

REALM OF THE ARCTIC FOX

⊙ HORNSTRANDIR

If you're looking for one of the last remaining true wildernesses in Europe, you need to look no further than Hornstrandir. This is the very northern tip of the Westfjords region, an uninhabited place that suffers through the very worst of Iceland's weather. The pyramid-shaped peaks have been sculpted by wind and ice, and giant cliffs stand defiantly against the raging Atlantic. In summer, when the snow has melted, the valleys run lush and green, home to rare plants, while birds flock to the cliffs.

This was once a place of small farms, with around 500 people living here in the 1930s. But without any roads or infrastructure of any kind, and long, cold winters, life was tough on the Horn. With the onset of World War II many farmers left for the capital, and the last hardy people to call Hornstrandir home left in 1952.

Since that time, the wildlife in Hornstrandir has reclaimed the land, and this is your best chance to encounter an arctic fox in the wild. They are the kings and queens of this landscape, and if you come hiking here in summer, you're all but guaranteed to spot a few. With the huge cliffs home to millions of nesting seabirds, there are plenty of food options and zero natural predators since the last Icelanders left.

Make no mistake though, this is a place of intense elements. Journeys here should only be undertaken by experienced hikers – or with a guide. Hornstrandir cops the brunt of the Arctic winds, with snow lingering in the shadows throughout summer and the nearby glacier making temperatures far colder than elsewhere in Iceland.

BELUGA WHALE SANCTUARY

⊙ VESTMANNAEYJAR (WESTMAN ISLANDS)

The Beluga Whale Sanctuary is a pioneering project aimed at providing a more natural habitat for captive beluga whales. This sanctuary, established by the Sea Life Trust in collaboration with the Whale and Dolphin Conservation (WDC), represents a significant step forward in marine mammal welfare. It officially opened in June 2019, welcoming two beluga whales, Little Grey and Little White, who were relocated from an aquarium in Shanghai.

The sanctuary is in a secluded cove in Klettsvik Bay, off Heimaey Island, the largest of the Vestmannaeyjar, where the population resides in town. The location was chosen for its ideal conditions for rehabilitating the whales, providing them with a better quality of life and allowing them to display more natural behaviours than they could in traditional aquariums.

Little Grey and Little White's journey to Vestmannaeyjar was complex and meticulously planned. It involved specialised transport equipment and a dedicated team of experts to ensure the whales' safety and well-being throughout the journey, which included a lengthy flight from China to Iceland. Now that they've arrived, they're thriving in their new habitat, which is offering a model for future projects.

Visiting the sanctuary provides visitors with a chance to learn about beluga whales and the importance of protecting marine life. It also underscores a growing recognition of the ethical implications of keeping such intelligent and social animals in captivity, representing a hopeful shift towards more humane treatment of marine mammals worldwide.

DON'T CALL THEM PONIES – A HISTORY OF THE ICELANDIC HORSE

⊙ AROUND ICELAND

Many people's enduring image of Iceland is a herd of horses thundering across a paddock, their long manes whipping in the winds, a glittering ice cap in the background. And you'll see plenty on your travels, particularly if you're journeying through West Iceland, the Snæfellsnes Peninsula, or North Iceland. The Icelandic horse is yet another example of Iceland's unique culture and historical heritage.

When the first settlers arrived in Iceland during the ninth and 10th centuries, they brought their horses. At first, they were most likely a mix of horses from Norway and the British Isles, but since Iceland was hugely isolated at the time, they were left largely untouched and developed into their own unique breed, forced to survive in the harsh environment. In 982, the Icelandic Alþing banned further importation of horses, and so for 1000 years, Icelandic horses were left to adapt to the unique conditions of their new home. And adapt they did. Whether carrying their Viking owners across a glacial river or crossing the vast deserts of the Highland plateau, they're uniquely suited to Iceland's

climate and weather. Today, the Icelandic horse is one of the purest breeds of horses in the world, with lineages that can be traced back to the Settlement Age. The breed is so unique that if one ever leaves the country, it's never allowed back in.

The horses' sturdy build ensures they can easily cross the country's rough landscapes, and in winter, their coats grow shaggy and long so they're unbothered by the biting winds. While other horses have only three gaits, the Icelandic horse has two additional gaits: the *tölt* and the flying pace. The *tölt* is comfortable, with one leg always on the ground, meaning there's no moment of suspension to bounce you in the saddle. When the horse adopts the flying pace, on the other hand, its two legs on one side move in unison, which lets the horse reach speeds of up to 50km/h (31mph).

Iceland's strict naming laws also govern the naming of Icelandic horses. A Naming Committee decides which names are acceptable or not, just like they do for the names of Icelanders themselves.

The beluga sanctuary in Klettsvik Bay
Opposite **A lone Icelandic horse**

"It's a unique opportunity for visitors to witness the community's dedication to preserving the local wildlife."

RESPONSIBLE
TRAVEL

Top **Out on Puffling Patrol**
Bottom **The Sea Life Trust Puffin Rescue Centre cares for lost puffins**

PUFFIN RESCUE

◉ VESTMANNAEYJAR (WESTMAN ISLANDS)

Each summer, the Atlantic puffin flocks to the rugged cliffs of Iceland to nest, raising their chicks in the protected holes that dot the cliff faces. Vestmannaeyjar (the Westman Islands), particularly Heimaey, is one of the top places to see these charming birds in summer (for more locations, *see* p. 68). As summer winds down, the puffins are drawn back out to sea, where they spend a long winter floating on the water and fishing. The chicks, known as pufflings, are also about to take off, but when they're ready to fly, they're often confused by the lights of Heimaey and fly into town instead of out to sea.

For about two weeks from mid-August to early September, the puffins leave the island, flying out to sea where they spend their winters on the water. During this time, locals stay out late at night, combing the streets of town on the lookout for lost pufflings. They find plenty too, on street corners, in fishing nets by the harbour and in backyards. They take them in overnight and release them out to sea the next day.

This heartwarming tradition, known as the Puffling Patrol, is a testament to the close relationship between the residents of Heimaey and the puffins. It's a unique opportunity for visitors to witness the community's dedication to preserving the local wildlife. If you're visiting near the end of August, keep your eyes peeled for any lost little pufflings in unsuspecting places, and let the experts know. It's a beautiful example of humans and nature attempting to coexist harmoniously, ensuring that the puffin population thrives for future generations to enjoy.

TREE PLANTING IN SOUTHERN ICELAND

◎ SMÁRATÚN FARM

One of the first things people will notice when travelling in Iceland is the distinct lack of trees. When the first settlers arrived, it's believed that around one-third of the country was covered in hardy birch forests – but these were swiftly chopped down to build boats and shelter, used as fuel to create tools and clear land for farms and their grazing livestock. But reforestation efforts have proven exceedingly difficult.

The first factor is the combination of Iceland's wind and volcanic soil. Iceland's soil is quite fine and easily carried away by the strong winds that so often buffer the country, leading to soil erosion that makes it hard for new trees to take root. And in summertime, the main season when they can absorb sunlight, free-roaming sheep love munching on baby birch saplings, hampering efforts.

Tree planting has become a tightly controlled challenge – but you can help. At Smáratún Farm, a small family-run guesthouse in the south, guests can help the reforestation efforts by planting trees on the farm. It's a great opportunity to learn more about the challenges of reforestation in Iceland and about the sustainability practices of the guesthouse itself. It's a leader in the region for sustainable tourism; the farm grows its own crops and raises horses, chickens, sheep, goats and more. It's even recognised by the Nordic Swan Ecolabel, the official eco-certification of the Nordic countries.

VERIÐ
VELKOMIN

SMARATÚN

GISTIHEIMLI-GUESTHOUSE
< SMAHYSI-CHALETS
BÍLAR-CAMPERVANS

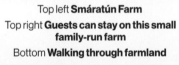

Top left **Smáratún Farm**
Top right **Guests can stay on this small family-run farm**
Bottom **Walking through farmland**

Top **An ICE-SAR lifeboat**
Bottom **ICE-SAR member navigates the snow on an ATV**

THE ICELANDIC SEARCH & RESCUE TEAM (ICE-SAR)

⊙ AROUND ICELAND

It's 2022, and my friends and I crest the top of a hill, nearing the volcanic eruption at Fagradalsfjall. Ahead of us, a man dressed in a bright red and blue jumpsuit turns towards us, revealing a gas mask covering his face. Like a scene from a sci-fi film, he waves a device in front of him slowly and methodically as it lets out a series of beeps. For a moment, he's framed by the red glow and smoke coming from the erupting volcano in the distance.

He's a member of the Icelandic Search and Rescue Team (ICE-SAR), monitoring the gas levels of the nearby eruption. With no wind, the gas is collecting at dangerous levels in the valley ahead of us. He points us to the mountain ridge on one side, indicating that we should do a big loop around the area before continuing to the eruption.

This is only a small part of the role played by members of ICE-SAR. A not-for-profit organisation operated entirely by local volunteers, Iceland's crack rescue squad is the best of the best when it comes to safety in Iceland's harshest conditions. Thanks to their highly specialised training, they're the experts in land and sea rescue operations when things go awry – as they so often do.

Whether it's an evacuation of a town due to a potential eruption or a complex rescue mission on a glacier in the middle of a howling blizzard, these are the Icelanders who risk their lives to save ours in a crisis.

The history of the ICE-SAR stretches back to 1918 when a small group of women banded together as a rescue team in case their husbands ran into trouble while fishing out at sea. Then, in 1950, when a plane crashed near Geysir and the American military failed in their rescue efforts, a crew of volunteer Icelanders executed a daring rescue in the harsh winter conditions, inspiring the nation. From that point onward, rescue teams popped up in different communities around the country, and ICE-SAR was established in 1999 to bring them all together under one organisation. Today, around 100 separate teams and thousands of volunteers are ready to help in the event of avalanches, storms, earthquakes, eruptions and anything else.

Donations to ICE-SAR help support this non-profit and volunteer organisation, which continues to protect and save lives within Iceland.

🔵 icesar.com

"Iceland offers a surprising natural bounty of ingredients that inform the country's growing reputation as a foodie destination."

FOOD & DRINK

FORAGED INGREDIENTS IN ICELAND — FROM LAND TO PLATE

◉ **AROUND ICELAND**

For a place just shy of the Arctic Circle, there's an abundance of ingredients that can be foraged in Iceland's unique volcanic landscapes. In the urban heart of Reykjavík, locals gather wild rhubarb and redcurrants growing in front gardens, while the vast countryside is a forager's paradise, offering wild berries, arctic herbs and elusive mushrooms.

The rise of New Nordic cuisine has seen Icelandic chefs embrace their local produce, and foraging is integral to this movement. Mussels cling to rocks on black-sand beaches, picked up alongside several different types of edible seaweed. In late summer, you might drive past a hill with several people combing the bushes for the wild berries that grow there. Meanwhile, any hot spots for mushrooms remain closely guarded secrets, known only to a fortunate few.

These ingredients are celebrated in modern Icelandic cuisine. Fresh Icelandic herbs enhance sauces and garnish dishes of lamb or fish. Berries, bursting with flavour, are a favourite for desserts, often accompanying the iconic skyr cheesecake. Mussels and mushrooms also feature prominently, reflecting the country's connection to both land and sea. This cast of foraged ingredients takes centre stage and enhances other Icelandic classics, all supported by fresh produce grown in the country's geothermal greenhouses.

Iceland offers a surprising natural bounty of ingredients that inform the country's growing reputation as a foodie destination.

Top **Berry-picking is common practice**
Bottom **An arctic char dish**

Top **Lamb**
Middle left **Arctic char**
Middle right **Plokkfiskur**
Bottom left **Hot dog**
Bottom right **Lobster soup**

ICELAND IN FIVE DISHES

⊙ REYKJAVÍK

Most people visit Iceland for the countryside, not the cuisine, but it's a surprisingly great destination for foodies. The New Nordic craze has swept across Reykjavík's restaurant scene, and alongside a renewed love for the local ingredients (grown in greenhouses and foraged), at most restaurants you'll find fanciful plates graced with arctic herbs, delicious and varied vegetarian options and inventive desserts. On top of that, an influx of immigrants also helps shape Iceland's foodie scene, opening restaurants and using Icelandic ingredients with their own traditional cooking methods. The result is a country on the cusp of becoming one of the world's best destinations for food.

Still, the classics are favourites for a reason. Here are five of Iceland's most famous dishes to keep your eyes peeled for.

A Leg of Lamb

Iceland's free-range lamb is a thing of legend – each summer, the country's sheep are set loose and free to roam anywhere they please. Thanks to this, free-range Icelandic lamb is one of the country's most famous meals – and one of the most expensive.

Catch of the Day

Fish, fish and more fish – there's no understating how important fish is for the average Icelander. This is a staple in restaurants, and ordering the catch of the day is always a good deal. Still, keep a special lookout for arctic char (Iceland's version of salmon) and brown trout, both caught in the expensive fishing rivers of Iceland.

Meat or Lobster Soup

Wind and rain hampering your explorations of Iceland? The country's go-to comfort food is a nice big bowl of soup that will warm you up. There are two specialties – the first is meat soup (*kjötsúpa*), with lamb, onion, cabbage, carrots, leeks and potatoes in a mouthwatering broth. The second is lobster soup (*humarsúpa*), a simple but delicious meal that's creamy and rich with delicious chunks of lobster hiding within.

Hot Dogs & Hamburgers

Icelanders love their hot dogs and hamburgers – something you'll discover very quickly. For hot dogs, there's only one place in Reykjavík you need to go to: Bæjarins Beztu Pylsur (*see* p. 90). Hamburgers are also wildly popular, a cultural hangover from when the Americans had a military base at Keflavík. There are countless spots in the capital to grab a juicy burger, and there are always veggie and vegan options as well.

Plokkfiskur

What started as a way to use up leftover fish has turned into one of the more popular traditional Icelandic meals. Plokkfiskur is a kind of fish stew mashed together with potatoes, milk, butter and cheese. It is best enjoyed with a still-warm slice of rye bread on the side and a healthy dollop of salted butter.

PYLSUR? JÁ TAKK!

⊙ BÆJARINS BEZTU PYLSUR, REYKJAVÍK

How did one little hot dog stand in Reykjavík become one of the city's biggest attractions? Nearly all travellers in Reykjavík make a stop at Bæjarins Beztu Pylsur (the town's best hot dogs), a small stand downtown that has been there since 1937. Iceland has a strong love for hot dogs, but it was a visit from Bill Clinton in 2004 that established the hot dogs from this stand as the best in the world. As he wandered nearby, the lady working the stand sang out to him: 'Best hot dogs in the world!'

'Why not?' said Bill, and ordered one hot dog with mustard only (an order which is now known as 'the Clinton'). An Icelandic photographer who was following Bill around that day snapped a photo, and in the following weeks Bæjarins Beztu Pylsur went on to become famous, culminating in a declaration from the *Guardian* in 2006 that it was one of the five best food stands to be found in Europe.

It has since been one of the major stops of any exploration of Reykjavík, including for visiting celebrities. Ben Stiller ate here when filming *The Secret Life of Walter Mitty,*

as did Metallica when they were in the city for a concert. Anthony Bourdain featured it on an episode of *No Reservations*, and even Kim Kardashian had a hot dog from here (ketchup only!).

So, what's so good about it? The combination of lamb, beef, and pork makes it a unique bite. Not many other hot dogs are made from lamb, and Icelandic lamb is among the best in the world. The other factor is the toppings. Order *ein með öllu* (one with everything), which is recommended by locals, and your dog will come topped with both crispy and fresh onions, mustard, ketchup and tomato sauce.

But it's not the only way to enjoy a hot dog. Reykjavík's biggest hot dog rival is Akureyri, which loads its up with all the trappings of a Reykjavík hot dog except with pickled red cabbage as well. And if you're anywhere near Stykkishólmur on the Snæfellsnes Peninsula, another hot dog stand is quickly gaining a reputation for itself: Meistarinn. Here they serve up delicious, deep-fried hot dogs with Doritos on top.

www.bbp.is

þjóðarr
ís

Bæjarins Beztu Pylsur,
home of hot dogs

Top **Tomato vines at Friðheimar**
Bottom **Friðheimar greenhouse**

GEOTHERMAL TOMATO FARM

⊙ FRIÐHEIMAR, REYKHOLT

Geothermal power in Iceland has been at the heart of the country's success for an age now, and visitors are often surprised to learn that Iceland grows its own fresh produce. The ability to harness geothermal power and use it in greenhouses allows Iceland to grow fresh tomatoes, cucumbers, cauliflower and even bananas – not to mention all kinds of fresh herbs.

One geothermal farm has not only succeeded at growing and selling produce but has also found success after pivoting toward tourism. Friðheimar is located in the small village of Reykholt in the Golden Circle region near Reykjavík and offers guests a glimpse at the inner workings of an Icelandic greenhouse. They do one thing, and they do it exceedingly well: tomatoes. If you buy any Icelandic tomatoes from the supermarket, chances are they were grown at Friðheimar.

Friðheimar has been in the family since the 15th century, and stopping to visit the farm is an experience – the restaurant is booked out months in advance. You'll see the tomatoes growing on their vines in the greenhouse, and then sit down at the table next to it to feast on – you guessed it – tomatoes. Pastas and pizza with homemade tomato sauces, tomatoes baked into bread and even tomato beer. When it comes to tomatoes, nothing is off limits at Friðheimar.

SUSTAINABLE SALT PRODUCTION IN THE WESTFJORDS

⊙ REYKJANES PENINSULA

A small sign with the word 'SALTVERK' painted in black is the only hint that there's something to see here. Behind the hotel set on the Reykjanes Peninsula in the Westfjords (not to be confused with the Reykjanes Peninsula in the south-west) sits a former fish factory turned sustainable salt factory.

Steam from the geothermal power rises along the shore, where rock pools collect – a mash-up of both seawater and boiling water. You can, of course, purchase the products at the supermarkets, but there's a nice touch to buying it directly from the location where it's made.

Inside, workers mill about boxing the product, including their two most popular varieties: lava salt and birch-smoked salt. We peek inside the smoking hut, enveloped in birch smoke as it rises over the flaky salt set in trays. In a connected building with windows overlooking the rough ocean

outside, seawater is pumped into large vats and heated with 93°C (206°F) water until it becomes a strong brine. Then, the geothermal water is used again to boil the brine until white crystals of salt eventually form on the surface and slowly fall to the bottom of the pan. It's then dried and packaged up or combined with activated charcoal (lava salt) or smoked over birch wood.

The Danish king was the one who first established salt production at this location in the 18th century, using geothermal energy to produce salt from the sea. But production only lasted a few decades, beginning again only in 2011 when Saltverk began operating with the geothermal waters on this small peninsula. Today, the high-quality and sustainable product is used at restaurants across Iceland, and their specialty salts make for a great souvenir for gourmet travellers.

🕭 saltverk.is

Top **Sustainably produced and high-quality salt**

Bottom **Seawater is pumped into large vats where it is heated to a strong brine**

Top **Coffee in Reykjavík**
Bottom **Kaffibrennslan**

COFFEE IN THE CAPITAL

⊙ REYKJAVÍK

Coffee is a serious business in Iceland, and as the capital, Reykjavík is the hub of all things caffeine. Whether you're after some good coffee to background your explorations around Reykjavík or you're looking for a quiet corner to soak up those hygge vibes, the following five cafes are celebrated in the city for their excellent grinds.

Reykjavík Roasters

Reykjavík Roasters (Kárastígur 1) is the most renowned coffee roaster in Iceland and has been at it since 2008 when it operated under the name Kaffismiðja Íslands. It imports high-quality coffee beans, is transparent about where it all comes from and roasts its imports with the utmost care to produce one of the best cups of coffee in Reykjavík.

Kaktus Espresso Bar

Cosy and warm with some sparse, bohemian-style interior decor, Kaktus (Vitastígur 12) was opened by two friends who serve the best Italian coffee in the capital. Mismatched wooden furniture, plenty of plants (cactus included) and a large window for watching the downtown action make Kaktus a great spot for some pared-back hygge vibes.

Kaffibrennslan

Kaffibrennslan (Laugavegur 21) is a cosy coffee spot inside a historic wooden house in the heart of Reykjavík. The creaky stairs and floorboards underneath enhance the Scandi atmosphere across the two-storey house, and the cafe is open late in case you're looking for a quiet refuge to enjoy a beer amid the madness of downtown Reykjavík on the weekend.

Plantan Kaffihús

A very vegan-friendly neighbourhood feel to Plantan Kaffihús (Njálsgata 64) makes this a favourite with locals in the downtown area. Enjoy the bright and plant-filled interior, and don't skip getting one of their cheese rolls. The owner is a photographer, so they have a real eye for detail when it comes to the decor, which is pared-back but stylish.

Kaffi Ó-Le

Kaffi Ó-le (Hafnastraeti 11) specialises in seasonal single-origin coffee, carefully sourced from farms. Industry veterans run this coffee shop, ensuring every delicate note is extracted from the beans. Enjoy the delicious coffee alongside fresh pastries and sandwiches with a healthy dose of calming Scandinavian vibes.

VEGETARIANS IN ICELAND

⦿ REYKJAVÍK

Fret not, it's not all fish and lamb on offer in Iceland. The country has taken great strides in becoming one of the most vegetarian-friendly destinations in Europe, and Reykjavík has several restaurants dedicated solely to vegetarian dishes. Here's where to go in the capital:

Garðurinn

Garðurinn (Klapparstígur 37), 'the Garden' in English, offers a variety of vegetarian and vegan dishes, with a small daily menu to choose from. Its cosy atmosphere and friendly service make it a delightful spot for plant-based meals, and the desserts are delicious.

Chickpea

This street-food-style takeaway eatery (Hallveigarstigur 1) specialises in falafel pita wraps and salads. It's been serving healthy and reasonably affordable Middle Eastern-inspired dishes since 2020 and has cemented its place among the top vegetarian restaurants in the city.

Hraðlestin

Hraðlestin (Hverfisgata 64A) is a family-run Indian restaurant with three locations around the capital. Established in 2003, it offers tasty, authentic Indian food at reasonable prices. The spices are directly imported from India and blended on-site. Expect plenty of vegetarian-friendly curries and other typical Indian dishes.

Kaffihús Vesturbæjar

Located about a 20-minute walk from downtown in the 107 neighbourhood, Kaffihús Vesturbæjar (Melhagi 20) is worth the stroll. This cafe has a distinctive local feel and several vegetarian items on its delicious menu. Try the vegan burger, made from portobello mushroom.

Mama Reykjavík

Mama Reykjavík (Bankastræti 2) is a restaurant and wellness space that focuses on creating a healthy and vibrant environment for guests not just to enjoy vegan food but also to rejuvenate their mind, body and soul. Keep an eye out for its events, which range from cacao ceremonies to live music.

Mama Reykjavík

Top **Waffles are a staple of the Westfjords**
Bottom **The cosy Litlibær Cafe**

WONDERFUL WAFFLES

⦿ WESTFJORDS

The far north-west corner of Iceland is home to a hardy population of locals, whose small towns cling to the edge of vast fjords. Waffles play a big role in powering self-supported cyclists in the Westfjords (see p. 134) and providing comfort on the often-blustery days. Here's where to set your sights for some golden and crispy waffles, like little rays of sunshine peeking out from behind the clouds to light up the larger-than-life scenery. Note that many of these places are only open in the warmer months.

Litlibær Cafe, Northern Westfjords

On the stretch of road dipping in and out of the northern fjords on the way to Ísafjörður is a historic 19th-century turf house called Litlibær. Once a farm, today it's an outpost for a hot cup of coffee and a plate of fluffy waffles, with a lookout nearby on the coast where you might spot seals and whales.

Nauteyri Steinshús

This is a small cafe themed around an old Icelandic poet called Steinn Steinarr, with a small display detailing his interesting biography. Located a small detour from the main road to Ísafjörður, the views from outside are phenomenal – as are the coffee and waffles.

Bókakaffi, Bolungarvík

Bolungarvík is about as far out as you can get in the Westfjords, a town north of Ísafjörður in a little-visited part of an already little-visited region. Here, a local bookstore serves up waffles in a cosy room filled with books to peruse, inviting you to linger for a while in one of the oldest fishing villages in Iceland.

Bryggjukaffi

A cafe located in the town of Flateyri, Bryggjukaffi is well-known in Iceland not just for its waffles, but also its homemade cakes, rhubarb jam and bagels. Locals drop by for lunch, and those who don't have time to linger can be seen filling to-go containers with fish soup.

Simbahöllin, Þingeyri

Located in Þingeyri, Simbahöllin is a beautiful, light-filled cafe that serves waffles, rents out bikes to travellers and celebrates the slow life. The historic house is beautiful, with creaky wooden floors inside, local flowers gracing small vases on the tables and superb views over the water. Down a plate of waffles before heading out to circle the Svalvogar Circle, a rough road that traces the edge of the peninsula.

BEER SAGAS IN ICELAND

⊙ AROUND ICELAND

Iceland has progressed in leaps and bounds with its beer in the past three decades. Considering that beer was banned in the country until 1989, the landscape of independent and big brewers on the scene today is impressive.

So, why was there a beer ban in Iceland? Much like the USA, there was a complete prohibition on alcohol in Iceland during the 20th century. That is until Spain complained to Iceland that they were importing fish from Iceland, but Iceland wasn't importing any wine from them. And so, the parliament decided that wine was OK, for the sake of their Spanish friends. The same thing went for spirits soon after. But beer, which was far cheaper than wine or spirits, remained prohibited since the government thought it would lead to an uptick in alcohol abuse. Beer was also strongly associated with the Danes, and with Iceland struggling for independence at the time, beer had a bit of a tarnished image.

But that doesn't mean that there wasn't any beer in Iceland. Ask an Icelander whose grandfather or great-grandfather was a ship captain, and you'll get the inside scoop on the lucrative off-market beer trade. Without extensive customs checks, fishing ships were free to bring whatever they liked back to Iceland from mainland Europe – mostly cases of beer that they stored in out-of-the-way sheds and garages, selling and gifting it to family, friends and others in town.

You could also buy low-percentage beer in Iceland (you still can in supermarkets today), which was often made more potent with a shot of vodka or Brennivín, the local Icelandic schnapps. But the sentiment shifted when travel opened up in the '60s and '70s, and Icelanders found themselves enjoying a nice beer at pubs in London. In 1980, it became legal for returning Icelanders to buy beer in the duty-free shop, a tradition still practised today as if it's a requirement. Finally, on 1 March 1989, beer was legalised completely, resulting in a nationwide party of epic proportions.

ICELAND'S BEST BREWERIES

✱ **RVK Brewing Company, Reykjavík** Located about half an hour's walk from downtown Reykjavík on the other side of Hlemmur is one of the capital's best breweries. RVK Brewing Company offers guided tours of its facilities (booking required) and also has a taproom where you can sample the creative craft beers.

✱ **Smiðjan Brugghús, Vík** Smiðjan Brugghús, located in the small industrial area of Vík, is one of the few breweries in South Iceland. Its offerings are delicious, and while it doesn't offer tours of the facilities, its beers can be enjoyed in their hipster-chic gastropub, pairing perfectly with the burgers and wings.

✱ **Beljandi Brewery, Breiðdalsvík** You'll find Beljandi Brewery in the blink-and-you'll-miss-it town of Breiðdalsvík, located in the East Fjords. The handcrafted beers here reflect the rugged and mountainous landscapes that make up this part of Iceland, which remains a very rural place. The brewery is only open in the warmer months, but if you're lucky enough to arrive on a busy night, you'll be rubbing shoulders with everyone from fishermen to reindeer hunters to Highland rangers.

✱ **Segull 67, Siglufjörður** Siglufjörður, located at the northernmost point of the Tröllaskagi Peninsula, was once among Iceland's busiest ports, driven by the thriving herring industry (*see* p. 162). Though the town has quieted since the herring stocks were depleted, tourism has provided some vital life to the town. Segull 67, a local brewery, now occupies an old harbour warehouse, where it welcomes visitors with tours and a cosy taproom to enjoy its craft beers.

✱ **Dokkan Brugghús, Ísafjörður** If you've made the long journey out to Ísafjörður, a stop at Dokkan Brewery is a must. Located amidst the large waterfront warehouses by the harbour, on a sunny day the terrace is the best place in town for a cheerful beer.

Dokkan Brugghús, the first brewery in the Westfjords

Top left **A hot chocolate with marshmallows, to go**
Top right **An egg and cheese bagel**
Bottom **The yellow school bus turned cafe**

COFFEE & COMMUNITY

⊙ SKOOL BEANS CAFE, VÍK

In the heart of Vík, Iceland, nestled between mountains and in the shadow of the Katla volcano (*see* p. 61), lies Skool Beans Cafe. Located inside a reformed yellow American school bus, it's one of the country's best spots for coffee, a unique micro-roaster and tea lab that has become a beloved gathering spot for locals and travellers passing through.

UK-born owner Holly Keyser spent six and a half years living in Melbourne and had become very familiar with the city's world-class coffee and cafe culture. On her way back home to the UK, she stopped over in Iceland to visit some friends but was quickly offered a job as a glacier guide. She decided she couldn't refuse the offer and stayed in the country, first living in the south-east before moving to Vík. But, during all this time, she was missing the comforts of having her own cafe, where baristas knew her order and she saw the staff members far more regularly than her own family. With nothing like that outside of Reykjavík, she decided to stop complaining and do something about it herself.

And so the idea behind Skool Beans came about; Holly wanted to create a space that could feel like a second home to others, a community-driven cafe for locals. Set to open in 2020, the pandemic threw a wrench in her plans, but she forged ahead with the opening. Doing so at a time when international tourism had completely shut down propelled her onto national news, but luckily, Icelanders were travelling extensively within their own country at the time. They came from all over to visit Skool Beans, meet with Holly and grab a takeaway coffee.

Despite the attention, it was still a tough year for Holly financially, made worse by her cat Jeffrey's leg injury. Fortunately, the community once again rallied behind her, crowdfunding enough money to have it treated and for Holly to push through to the other side of the pandemic.

The tight-knit community in Vík welcomed Skool Beans with open arms. Holly had lived in the village for some time before opening, so the locals knew her and what she was about. She wasn't there just to capitalise on tourism in the area but rather to add something valuable to the community. Since then, the yellow bus in Vík has seen proposals and impromptu live music performances and continues to act as a meeting place for locals as well as one of the best spots for coffee in Iceland.

Follow Holly on Instagram @skool_beans, and for fans of cats, check out @sirjeffarious. Just don't try to pat him while he's eating.

HOT PLATES, COOL WATER

⊙ LAKE MÝVATN

Lake Mývatn in North Iceland is a volcanic wonderland, sitting in the middle of the Krafla volcanic system. This series of fissures and magma chambers beneath the surface has shaped the area into one of Iceland's volcanic hot spots with craters, steaming hot springs, lava fields and Mars-like landscapes.

But there's a side to the volcanic energy that visitors don't see: the food. A private geothermal bakery that remains off limits to visitors churns out delicious *rúgbrauð* (rye bread) cooked underground by volcanic steam. You can find the bread on offer at restaurants around the lake, in the hotels and at the cafe of the Mývatn Nature Baths hot spring. Most serve it with a healthy dollop of salted Icelandic butter or with a slice of Arctic char on top, the salmon-like fish that's one of the most popular in Iceland.

That's not the only local produce you'll feast on around the lake. At Vogafjós Farm Resort, the farm-to-table dining experience is taken very seriously; diners can gaze through a window at the restaurant into the next-door cowshed as they eat fresh mozzarella, slow-cooked lamb and local beef, emphasising the importance of knowing where your food comes from. Vogafjós's commitment to zero-kilometre food and sustainability has earned them a badge with Vakinn, Iceland's official quality and environmental rating system for tourism.

Fish is also a big part of the Icelandic diet, and locals have plied the waters of Lake Mývatn since the first settlers arrived back in the ninth century. Today, commercial fishing is limited to 14 days every summer to ensure that fishing in the lake remains sustainable, but locals are allowed to fish year-round. Farmers instead purchase local Arctic char from nearby aqua farms at Húsavík – the fish is a favourite in Iceland and a staple of the diet around the lake. Pan-fried Arctic char at Lake Mývatn is likely to be some of the best fish you'll eat in the country, and if you're lucky, you might even score some that were plucked out of the lake itself. Locals will tell you there's nothing better than the Arctic char caught from the lake. Fat brown trout are also local to the lake, feeding on the swarms of midges that descend on the basin each summer (Mývatn is Icelandic for 'Midge Lake'). Often, you'll be able to try pieces of trout smoked over lamb dung, a traditional dish in the area.

Lamb, too, is a big dish of Lake Mývatn, with restaurants purchasing it from farmers across northern Iceland. And then there are the fresh vegetables grown in nearby geothermal greenhouses, providing a surprising abundance of produce to grace and garnish plates. Like many other things in Iceland, the lambs are direct descendants of the first sheep to arrive with the Vikings. It has been a traditional dish in the country since the beginning, and Lake Mývatn is one of the best destinations to get a feel for the traditional foods and cooking methods.

Top **Lake Mývatn trout**

Bottom **Bjarnarflags Brauð** is baked in Lake Mývatn's hot springs

The steaming geothermal vents of Lake Mývatn

"Floats, costumes, music and dance create a carnival-like atmosphere that spreads love and acceptance."

FESTIVALS & EVENTS

ICELANDIC NATIONAL DAY

⊙ AROUND ICELAND

Iceland's National Day, celebrated on 17 June, is the most important holiday in the country, commemorating Iceland's independence from Denmark in 1944. This significant date is closely tied to the life and efforts of Jón Sigurðsson, the 'Father of Independence'.

Jón Sigurðsson, an educated Icelander, played a pivotal role in the independence movement. Living in Denmark, he worked in the Icelandic literature section of Copenhagen University. Jón and his colleagues launched Fjölnir, a journal of Icelandic essays and arguments that would go on to become the cornerstone of Iceland's independence movement. It provided a platform for intellectual discourse and championed the country's fight for independence from Denmark.

However, Iceland's journey toward independence began long before Jón's time. In 930, the country declared itself a commonwealth on the plains of Þingvellir, establishing a system of universal laws. By 1220, power had consolidated into the hands

of six wealthy families, leading to bloody battles and family feuds. King Hákon of Norway exploited these conflicts, eventually making Iceland a subject of Norway in 1262.

Norway's fate was tied to Denmark in 1397, when a pact placed both nations under the Danish Crown, and Iceland remained under Danish rule for centuries. The 18th century brought a wave of revolutionary fervour from Europe, inspiring Icelandic intellectuals in Copenhagen to push for independence. Jón Sigurðsson emerged as a leader among these intellectuals, using Fjölnir to rally support and articulate the case for sovereignty.

Denmark, feeling the pressure, gradually granted more rights to Iceland. The tipping point came during World War II when the Nazi occupation of Denmark allowed Iceland to assert its independence. Jón Sigurðsson's legacy lived on as Iceland declared its independence on his birthday, 17 June, in 1944.

CELEBRATE LIKE A LOCAL

If you're in Reykjavík for Iceland's National Day, head downtown to experience a carnival-like atmosphere with parades, marching bands, street theatre, folk dances and live music.

Top **The Icelandic flag**
Bottom **Families and friends celebrate Icelandic National Day**

Top **Ísafjörður commemorates the fishermen and women who lost their lives at sea**

Bottom **Training sessions**

SJÓMANNADAGURINN – FISHERMEN'S DAY

⊙ WESTFJORDS & EASTFJORDS

Iceland has long had an important relationship with the sea, and Sjómannadagurinn is the celebration of all the fishermen and women, past and present, who take to the seas. While Iceland's modern fishing fleet offers those on-board sleek facilities with private ensuite cabins, high-speed wi-fi, and access to live football matches, it wasn't always this way. Not so long ago, it was one of the most dangerous professions in Iceland, with fishermen forced to contend with the elements and fierce storms.

As such, it makes sense that Fishermen's Day is a big celebration in Iceland, honouring some of the country's hardest workers.

Wherever you are around the country, you can be sure there's a celebration happening on this day, but the biggest and best parties happen in the Westfjords and Eastfjords, within the communities where fishing is still thriving. Think Patreksfjörður, Ísafjörður and Bolungarvík in the Westfjords, while in the Eastfjords stop by Neskaupstaður or Eskifjörður for the most fun.

Activities range from huge tug-of-wars with anchor rope to live music to free boat rides out at sea. And, of course, there's a healthy dose of competition as well, with rowing, swimming and even pillow fights on logs floating on the water, all drawing big crowds.

RÉTTIR – ANNUAL SHEEP ROUND-UP

⊙ AROUND ICELAND

Drive through Iceland in summer and you'll see thousands of sheep scattered across the landscape. From June, farmers let them roam freely with their young lambs in tow, and it's remarkable how often you'll come across a sheep in the oddest of places. It seems they cover more ground than hikers on the Laugavegur Trail when they are roaming the countryside in search of some choice grass.

Of course, the tricky part comes when it's time to round them up again. September is when the Réttir takes place, or the round-up. This is when Icelanders mount their horses and ride off into the countryside to round up any sheep. And because they've wandered off into the darndest of places (perched on vertical cliff faces, on small islands found in lakes and in the remotest corners of the highlands), it's all a bit of an adventure for everyone involved. The sheep are corralled back down to the lowlands, then herded into a pen where the families sort out who belongs to whom, and everyone goes on their merry way – the key word being merry since there's a lot of drinking involved as well.

Legends tell of sheep that have gone missing, only to turn up munching on grass in the Highlands next summer, a pair of new lambs in tow. And like most industrious Icelanders, farmers have made it a profitable venture, welcoming tourists onto farmsteads where they stay, drink, eat and help round up the sheep (or more than likely get in the way). It's a great opportunity to spend time in corners of the country you wouldn't otherwise think about visiting.

Top **Corralling a flock of sheep**
Bottom **Sheep-sorting on the Réttir**

Westman Island's Festival is one of Iceland's most famous events

WESTMAN ISLAND'S FESTIVAL

⊙ VESTMANNAEYJAR (WESTMAN ISLANDS)

I'm sitting next to my partner on the hillside, watching as several huge bonfires are lit above us. The stage in front has a single singer and guitar player, while the hillside comes alive with a chorus of song as Icelandic people sing along to the songs. This is the culmination of the Westman Island's Festival (Þjóðhátíð), and afterwards, hundreds of people on the clifftop above light their torches and hold them aloft, recreating the Eldfell eruption that happened on the island in 1973. The previous nights were hedonistic. On the Friday night, a huge bonfire provided warmth to the entire area as the latest and greatest Icelandic artists took to the stage. By the second night, the atmosphere had transformed, and I found myself in a writhing mosh pit while DJs and a famous Icelandic funk rock group fuelled the crowd's energy. Come Monday morning, the chaos of the festival lingers. People are sprawled on the deck of the ferry back to the mainland, catching up on sleep wherever they can, and a long queue of cars wait to turn onto the ring road and head back to the capital, held up by the police issuing breathalyser tests.

This is Iceland's most famous festival, but only among Icelanders themselves. A rite of passage for locals, for three days in August they'll camp near the natural amphitheatre on Vestmannaeyjar (the Westman Islands), meet with friends, watch live music and generally have a raucous good time. It takes place on the same weekend that most of the country is celebrating a public holiday, but this is by far the best celebration in the country. Locals from Heimaey set up huge white tents where you can cosy up from the cold and meet other festival-goers, drink and eat; there's a line-up full of Iceland's hottest artists and bands and a huge fireworks show that rivals New Year's Eve in Reykjavík (*see* p. 124). It's such a big deal that every year an Icelandic artist is selected to write a unique anthem for the festival, which is played to death on radio stations in the lead-up. Þjóðhátíð is tradition and reckless abandon, and an all-too-real taste of just how hard Icelanders can party.

🌀 dalurinn.is

ICELAND AIRWAVES

⊙ REYKJAVÍK

Iceland Airwaves is a renowned music industry conference, showcase and festival that takes over Reykjavík for a weekend at the beginning of November. Despite other festivals fading away in recent years, Airwaves remains Iceland's premier music festival, attracting international acts to the capital. For one weekend, the festival spotlights up-and-coming artists, celebrates established favourites and fosters extensive networking among industry professionals, from radio stations to booking agents to musicians.

Rex Beckett and Jóhannes Bjarkason, music journalists at the *Reykjavík Grapevine*, Iceland's largest English-language publication covering travel, life and entertainment, provide an insider's perspective on Iceland's biggest music festival.

'Airwaves is so special, thanks in huge part to its location in Reykjavík,' says Rex, a Canadian transplant who arrived in 2010 and never left. She's a seasoned pro with experience performing at the festival and reporting on it for the *Grapevine*. 'Those early years were chaotic. You could really feel this special atmosphere throughout the city, with music wafting out of every bar.'

Iceland is known for its outstanding creativity, with the local music scene being a significant part of that reputation. 'When we think about our history, I think we really underestimate how crucial creative elements are for the survival of our species,' says Rex. 'It has always been a way to keep your spirits up, keep you connected with your community. I think that's why Icelanders are so creative. They've historically had to be self-reliant; they not only had to catch their own fish to survive but also knit their clothes and entertain themselves with music and art. I think creativity in Iceland is so prevalent because Icelanders had to be to survive back in the day when they were hunkered down for the winter.'

Jóhannes Bjarkason, who has also performed at the festival, fulfilled a long-held dream that began when he first attended as a teenager. Along with Rex, he hosts the music podcast *66 Degrees of Sound*, covering new Icelandic music releases in English.

'The festival has changed a lot over the past decade. It's still a time when the whole city comes alive, and you can wander through the streets and hear music coming out of every second bar downtown. But it's also different now. The off-venues are strictly controlled now, so not anyone can just throw an impromptu gig at any old bar,' says Jóhannes.

Off-venues were a unique aspect of Iceland Airwaves, allowing venues not officially part of the festival to host bands in town. Anyone in the city could visit an off-venue, giving even those not attending the festival a taste of the music scene. Nowadays, Iceland Airwaves strictly controls who can become an off-venue and manages the line-ups. However, in an example of true Icelandic resilience, there are ways around it. 'We held an off-venue event, but we just didn't have Iceland Airwaves in the event name to avoid getting sued. We organised a gig of grassroots Icelandic artists who we thought should have been on the official line-up that year,' says Jóhannes.

Iceland Airwaves continues to be a vital event in Reykjavík's cultural calendar, showcasing the city's vibrant music scene and fostering a sense of community and creativity. Whether you're an industry professional or a music enthusiast, this festival offers a unique and unforgettable experience in the heart of Iceland.

🌐 icelandairwaves.is

Top **Musicians take to the Iceland Airwaves stage**
Bottom **An array of Iceland's musical talent is showcased at the event**

Top **Mischievous Yule Lads**
Bottom **Modern Yule Lads are generally well-behaved**

THE MISCHIEVOUS YULE LADS – CHRISTMAS IN ICELAND

⦿ AROUND ICELAND

Come Christmas time in Iceland, rather than just being paid a visit by Santa Claus, Icelandic children are blessed with 13 different characters who drop off presents. Known as the Icelandic Yule Lads, this group of mischievous characters aren't quite as well-behaved as old Father Christmas. Each has a distinct personality and a unique way of stirring up holiday shenanigans. Here's a list of them and their antics:

1. **Sheep-Cote Clod:** He tries to suckle ewes in farmer's sheep sheds.
2. **Gully Gawk:** He steals foam from buckets of cow milk.
3. **Stubby:** He's short and steals food from frying pans.
4. **Spoon Licker:** He licks spoons.
5. **Pot Scraper, aka Pot Licker:** He steals unwashed pots and licks them clean.
6. **Bowl Licker:** He steals bowls of food from under the bed.
7. **Door Slammer:** He stomps around and slams doors, keeping everyone awake.
8. **Skyr Gobbler:** He eats up all the Icelandic yogurt (*skyr*).
9. **Sausage Swiper:** He loves stolen sausages.
10. **Window Peeper:** He likes to creep outside windows and sometimes steal the stuff he sees inside.
11. **Door Sniffer:** He has a huge nose and an insatiable appetite for stolen baked goods.
12. **Meat Hook:** He snatches up any meat left out, especially smoked lamb.
13. **Candle Beggar:** He steals candles, which used to be sought-after items in Iceland.

Despite all this mischief, these characters do drop off presents. Every night in the lead-up to Christmas Eve, Icelandic children leave their shoes on windowsills, waking in the morning to find a present inside. And if they've been naughty? A rotten potato or two. But those children who have behaved extra naughty have to contend with Grýla, mother of the Yule Lads, an evil troll who comes down from the mountains on Christmas to boil naughty children alive in her large cauldron. There's also a bloodthirsty black cat called the Christmas Cat who will eat those who don't receive a new piece of clothing before Christmas.

Since 1746, parents have been officially banned from tormenting their children with these Christmas monsters, and as a result, today, the Yule Lads are generally well-behaved and harmless.

NEW YEAR'S EVE – COMEDY & FIREWORKS

⊙ AROUND ICELAND

Iceland loves a good party on New Year's Eve. While many European destinations have official fireworks shows at a designated location, Icelanders are let loose to purchase as many fireworks as they please to let off at midnight. The result is a countrywide showcase of huge colourful explosions as the clock strikes midnight; the skies are filled with fireworks of all sizes and power.

Before the big moment though, it's tradition for Icelanders to gather at bonfires in the early evening. Then, for an hour between 11pm and midnight, the streets empty as nearly everyone heads inside to watch what's known as the Áramótaskaup. This is the traditional New Year's Eve comedy show, where Icelandic comedians, actors and musicians create funny sketches and songs based on the top news stories, scandals and events that happened throughout the year. It's one of the most highly anticipated moments of the evening.

And after the Áramótaskaup finishes with a special song written just for the show, it's fireworks time. Most Icelanders will spend the evening with families and head outside to set off whatever fireworks they could afford in the weeks leading up to the big night. It must be experienced to be believed; if you're in Reykjavík, the main square in front of Hallgrímskirkja Church is one of the busiest places.

REYKJAVÍK INTERNATIONAL FILM FESTIVAL

◎ **REYKJAVÍK**

Opposite **Reykjavík is known for its New Year's Eve fireworks**
Top **Filmmakers present their work**

Iceland's landscapes have long captivated the imaginations of filmmakers worldwide, and this profound connection with cinema is celebrated annually at the Reykjavík International Film Festival (RIFF). The festival, held every year in late September or early October, is a strong reminder of Iceland's importance in the global film industry and is a natural extension of Iceland's relationship with international production companies who have used the country's landscapes for film and television.

The list of major movies and TV series filmed in Iceland is long. Think projects like *Game of Thrones*, *Interstellar*, *The Secret Life of Walter Mitty*, and *True Detective*,

all of which have showcased the dramatic scenery in Iceland to great effect. But at RIFF, independent and up-and-coming filmmakers take centre stage.

These emerging directors show off their films at venues across Reykjavík, but also in unique locations in Iceland. Horror films have been screened inside caves, dramas at local swimming pools and even a climate-change documentary inside an ice cave on Langjökull Glacier. It's a unique way to tie together cinema with the natural attractions of Iceland and a beautiful celebration of independent work in a country that has been working with the big guns for decades.

🔗 riff.is

Top **Celebrating Reykjavík Pride**
Bottom **Pride flag waving at the Pride Parade**
Opposite **A Reykjavík street dolled up for Pride**

REYKJAVÍK PRIDE

REYKJAVÍK

Reykjavík Pride is the country's biggest and most vibrant celebration of the LGBTQIA+ community. Held annually in August, the week-long festival turns the capital city into a hub of parades, concerts, cultural events and educational programs. What began as a modest gathering back in 1999 has grown into one of the most anticipated events on the city's calendar and attracts thousands of participants and visitors from around the world.

Like most Pride events, the heart of Reykjavík Pride is the Pride Parade, a spirited procession through downtown. Floats, costumes, music and dance create a carnival-like atmosphere that spreads love and acceptance. Workshops, lectures and art exhibitions held throughout the city during Pride also educate and engage the wider public, addressing various aspects of LGBTQIA+ history and rights.

This crucial event in Reykjavík fosters a strong culture of acceptance in a country already famous for its progressive stance on LGBTQIA+ issues. Iceland was the first country to elect an openly gay head of state, Jóhanna Sigurðardóttir, who served as the prime minister between 2009 and 2013.

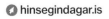 hinsegindagar.is

"Venture into the furthest reaches of Iceland's coastline, seeking out the most epic swell"

ACTIVITIES & SPORTS

FEELING THE HEAT – ICELAND'S VOLCANOES & THE LAVA SHOW

⊙ REYKJAVÍK & VÍK

Iceland is truly a dream destination for amateur volcanologists. And aren't we all exactly that? The spectacle of an eruption is awe-inspiring, a vivid reminder of nature's power. In Iceland, that experience is up close and personal. This is a country with a smouldering core, where magma pulses beneath the craggy landscapes and ice caps, spewing forth from rifts and fissures and sculpting new terrain. It's an unparalleled destination for volcano enthusiasts.

And now, there's a place in Iceland to witness molten lava up close: the Lava Show. 'We had the idea to show off lava in a controlled environment after witnessing the largest lava fall in recorded history when there was an eruption at Fimmvörðuháls in 2010,' says Ragga, who, along with her husband Júlíus, is the brains behind the Lava Show. That 2010 eruption sent lava oozing over a mountain ridge, plummeting about 200m (650ft) off the cliff to the ground below. 'It was an indescribable experience for us, looking at this towering flow of lava. We thought to ourselves, how can we capture this feeling and share it with the rest of the world?'

Their answer to that question is the Lava Show, where an advanced furnace heats up lava rocks until they liquefy back into their molten state. That lava is then poured down a chute into a room full of amazed onlookers, watching on in awe as a presenter

endures the sweltering heat to manipulate the lava with a long metal rod – lifting, overturning and eventually breaking it open when it cools to show the glowing, fiery core. 'We think of it as edutainment – part education, part entertainment. People are often shocked when the lava first comes out. I remember when we first began, people didn't believe it was real,' says Ragga.

It's one of the more obvious volcanic tourism experiences in a country brimming with explosive spectacle. Iceland's primordial landscapes have hypnotised tourists following the 2010 Eyjafjallajökull eruption, which unleashed a colossal ash cloud leading to the most extensive air traffic shutdown since World War II. Major eruptions are behind most of what makes Iceland so tempting, pooling into dark fields of lava, scoring mountains with hues of red, orange and yellow, and eroding into black-sand beaches on the coast and wind-whipped deserts in the interior. Beneath the ice caps, volcanic activity triggers monumental glacial floods, surging forth to carve out canyons and give rise to thunderous waterfalls.

And it's not just the aftermath of eruptions that spark interest, but eruptions themselves. Thanks to a handful of visitor-friendly eruptions occurring on the Reykjanes Peninsula, just a short drive from Reykjavík, seeing molten lava spewing forth from a fissure has become a reality for many. Scientists predict this volcanic zone is entering an era of heightened activity, but that's a cause for concern. This is Iceland's most populated corner, meaning significant risk to homes and livelihoods if an eruption threatens towns or critical infrastructure. 'Eruptions can be amazingly beautiful, but also devastating,' says Ragga.

Whether it's a real-life volcanic eruption, watching lava in the controlled environment of the Lava Show or exploring the volcanically sculpted terrain, Iceland presents an opportunity to experience the fascinating – and frightening – power of volcanoes.

The Lava Show (icelandiclavashow.com) has daily demonstrations in both Reykjavík and Vík.

Top **Lava flows from the Eyjafjallajökull volcano**
Bottom **The Lava Show**

FIVE MORE VOLCANIC ACTIVITIES IN ICELAND

The Thríhnúkagígur Lava Chamber – Capital Area

This is the only place on Earth where you can descend into a dormant volcano and explore its giant lava chamber. Usually, lava solidifies after an eruption, but here it's like someone pulled the plug instead. It's likely that the lava seeped back down towards the Earth's core, leaving behind the gigantic chamber, which could fit the Statue of Liberty inside with room to spare.

Krafla, Leirhnjúkur & Hverir – North Iceland

In North Iceland, the area around Lake Mývatn is home to a collection of fascinating volcanic phenomena. There's the Krafla volcanic crater filled with milky blue water and the still-steaming Leirhnjúkur lava field. The geothermal power of the place is also on full display at Hverir, an area of Mars-like landscapes, belching mud pots and steam gushing from vents in the earth.

Hike the Fimmvörðuháls Pass – South Iceland

Location of the lava fall that inspired Ragga and Júlíus, the Fimmvörðuháls Pass is a popular day trek between the waterfall Skógafoss and the Þórsmörk Nature Reserve. It can also be added to the longer Laugavegur Trek, Iceland's most famous multiday hike between Landmannalaugar and Þórsmörk.

Snæfellsjökull National Park – West Iceland

One of the few cone-shaped volcanoes in Iceland, the Snæfellsjökull ice cap and volcano sits at the very tip of the Snæfellsnes Peninsula at the heart of its own national park. Here, lava fields spill into the ocean, twisted coastal cliffs, giant volcanic craters and windswept black-sand beaches.

Askja Volcanic Caldera – Highlands

A far-flung corner of Iceland's wilderness, located north of Vatnajökull, is the Askja Volcanic Caldera. The landscape here bears the scars of the nation's most violent eruptions, with huge craters, battered lava fields and Víti, a crater lake filled with chalky water warm enough for a dip.

Top **Ash clouds after an Eyjafjallajökull eruption**

Bottom **Volcanic eruption on the Reykjanes Peninsula**

BY STEAM, SPOKE & SADDLE – BIKING THE NORTH-WEST

⊙ THE WESTFJORDS WAY

Land, sea, wind, water and ice – such is the nature of Iceland's remote north-western corner, a place of remarkable beauty that most travellers pass by completely. Far removed from the rest of the country, there's a certain magic about the Westfjords. This is technically the oldest part of Iceland, a place of deep valleys and flat-topped mountains, all of which are carved out by extinct glaciers. Overlooked by most in lieu of a trip around the ring road, there's one group of travellers who are increasingly drawn by the sheer beauty and remoteness: cyclists.

No crowds, larger-than-life scenery, unique culture and hardly any car traffic on the roads all combine to make the Westfjords a popular spot for cyclists. In recent years, a new multi-stage endurance race – the Arna Westfjords Way Challenge – has not only tempted new travellers to the region but also helped boost the local economy.

'In 2021, I received a grant to cycle around the Westfjords and analyse it for biking infrastructure. Like, where can you get help here if you're travelling by bike?' says Tyler Wacker, an American who settled in Ísafjörður after having studied Coastal Communities and Regional Development at the university there. He's one part of Cycling Westfjords, the organisation that has taken charge of the race since its inception by a group of cyclists employed by the regional tourism office to help publicise the route after it was announced.

'I got to ride with them for two days, and during that time the idea for the race came together,' he says.

A big part of that idea involved intertwining the cycling stages with tourism development in the Westfjords. Riders can receive a time reduction on each stage of the race by stopping off at what's called a 'cultural connection'. Cyclists must stop by at least two cultural connections during each stage, clocking out of the race to soak in a hot spring, check out a museum, visit a local farm or simply take it easy at a cafe. This concept ties the entire race together; it brings in a diversified income for local businesses and fosters a deeper connection with the Westfjords for the race participants.

'My favourite one is the first stop, at a place called Litlibær. It's this small cafe in a 19th-century turf house. It's the first cultural connection, so everyone arrives there at pretty much the same time. Then it's just this party vibe at the small cafe, and they're slinging waffles out of the window, and everyone's pumping in coffee for the rest of the day,' says Tyler.

The caffeine kick surely helps for what's to come, with cyclists tackling gruelling stages over the next few days that take them in and out of fjords, over mountain passes and along rough, gravel roads. Then, there's the weather. Biting wind and rain are commonplace in the Westfjords, even during summer. Luckily, local guesthouses and hotels act as warm refuges each evening, complete with coffee, cakes and sometimes even a talking raven.

'One time a cyclist was just so cold he had to stop racing. But luckily, he was quite close to a farm. He knocked on their door and they welcomed him inside for dinner, which had just hit the table. And I just think – there aren't many other places in Iceland where something like that could happen,' says Tyler.

Only around 7000 people live in the Westfjords, with small farms and villages tucked away in the fjords at a great distance from one another. This also means that cyclists are more inclined to stop in each town for a break, getting to know the local culture and residents who call this part of Iceland home better than most other travellers.

'Our dream would be to attract more bike travellers than cars to the Westfjords. It really feels like one of the last places where you can slow down and take your time travelling. No one is in a rush around here,' says Tyler. The Westfjords Way is much more than simply the route of the race. It's also the way of the people here.

The Arna Westfjords Way Challenge takes place in the Westfjords every June. Cycling Westfjords (cyclingwestfjords.com) also helps travellers organise their routes, providing route advice, luggage transportation and unbeatable local recommendations.

Top **Látrabjarg cliffs, Westfjords**
Bottom **Bikepacking along Westfjords Way**

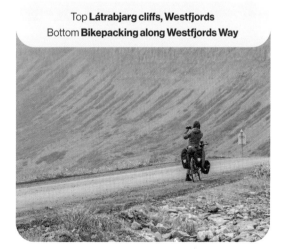

Cyclists ride through
Vesturland

SOUTH COAST PARAGLIDING & ZIPLINES

◉ VÍK

Iceland's south coast, renowned for its dramatic landscapes and natural beauty, is also where visitors can jump on paragliding and zipline tours. Vík has become a hot spot for adventure tours and the place to go for travellers looking for unique experiences.

Paragliding over the south coast is an exhilarating way to experience this stunning part of the country. The expansive black-sand beaches and fierce ocean tides have historically prevented the development of many settlements along the coast, leaving a pristine landscape. Soaring above on a paragliding tour, you'll appreciate the stark contrasts between the black sands, verdant green rolling hills and gleaming white glaciers.

Those glaciers, Eyjafjallajökull and Mýrdalsjökull, have also contributed to the region's dramatic terrain. Both ice caps hide volcanoes beneath, and eruptions have carved out steep gorges, jagged canyons and rushing glacial rivers. Ziplining through the landscape is a straightforward way to appreciate the natural beauty of Iceland's south coast region without having to contend with the huge crowds you'll find at major sights. Meanwhile, electronic mountain bike tours also let you explore far deeper than many other travellers.

And when all is said is done, back in Vík, you can warm up with a hot coffee and pastry from Skool Beans (*see* p. 105), a charming cafe housed in a reformed yellow American school bus.

🌐 trueadventure.is

Top **Ziplining takes your time in Vík to new heights**

Bottom **Paragliding over Skógafoss**

Paragliding over the top of
Iceland's south coast

Diving between two
tectonic plates at Silfra

PLUNGING BETWEEN THE PLATES

◉ SILFRA

Iceland is precariously perched above two tectonic plates, slowly inching away from each other at the rate of 2cm (0.8in) a year. There are places where you can see this rift – on the Reykjanes Peninsula, at Þingvellir National Park and around Lake Mývatn – but there's only one spot where you can dive into the rift: Silfra.

This is the name of the section of the Mid-Atlantic Ridge that plunges beneath the surface of Lake Þingvellir, created when an earthquake shifted the ground back in 1789. This seismic activity opened several of the fissures you see today around Þingvellir, but it was Silfra that immediately captured the most attention. The fissure is fed by meltwater from the nearby glacier Langjökull, but not through a river. Instead, the water finds its way underground, filtering through underground lava rocks for between 30 and 100 years, and finally spilling out into the fissure via an underwater spring. This constant inflow of fresh spring water means that in winter the water doesn't freeze; it also means that you can take off your mask to take a big gulp of some fresh, lava-filtered glacial water.

This rocky channel is an adventure like no other. For starters, the water here is clearer than pretty much anywhere else in the world, due to the natural filtering. Seeing over 100m (330ft) down to the clear sandy bottom is vertigo-inducing for some. The basalt cliffs and untouched sandy bottom below are decorated with strange algae, glowing pink, purple and green. The other striking thing about the fissure is the complete lack of marine life.

Silfra is a 'living' dive site, so it is constantly changing. In addition to the tectonic plates inching away from each other each year, earthquakes in the region also cause boulders to shift and fall, sometimes resulting in new underwater tunnels to explore.

🜄 dive.is

THE BEAST OF THE EAST — GLACIAL RIVER RAFTING

◎ **VARMAHLÍÐ**

A rushing river of glacial meltwater churns between the canyon walls, a tumultuous world of freezing water and rugged, basalt cliffs. In this hidden and wild corner of north Iceland, the river Austari Jökulsá (East Glacial River in English) is the queen of all things. Free-flowing from the northern edge of Hofsjökull, a glacier in the central Highlands, the river carves through 50km (31 miles) of the remote countryside before channelling into a spectacular 15km (9-mile) gorge. And come summer, when the warmer weather sends a surge of glacial meltwater downstream, it's raging at full power.

Located about 30 minutes south of Varmahlíð in North Iceland, the gorge offers a stunning section of Class IV rapids. That makes it one of the most extreme stretches of river in all of Europe, but the churning water is also interspersed with stretches of calm, essential to let you admire the surrounding scenery. And it is incredible: tall basalt cliffs rising on each side, sections of gravel etched in colourful reds and oranges indicating past geothermal power and green moss clinging to craggy cliffs. Rocks and water are two of the things that Iceland does best, and there's no better way to experience the two than with a whitewater rafting tour.

Some tours venture down the Vestari Jökulsá (West Glacial River) for those looking for something more relaxing. The river spills into two separate canyons, and the western canyon is ideal for family-style rafting. The towering gorge around you twists and turns, with riverside hot springs and gentle rapids.

◍ vikingrafting.is

144

Top **The raging glacial meltwater makes for an exciting rafting experience**

Bottom **Slightly calmer waters and majestic scenery**

THE SPORT OF *SPRANGA*

⊙ VESTMANNAEYJAR (WESTMAN ISLANDS)

S*pranga* is a daring form of cliff jumping, and one of Iceland's more unique and challenging traditions. Born and practised in Vestmannaeyjar, *spranga* originated as a skill for locals who needed to collect bird eggs from the sheer cliffs that ring the island landscape. But it's not as simple as scaling a cliff face attached to a rope. Participants propel themselves outwards with their feet, swooping across the cliff face and grabbing onto different rocky outcrops when they land. It's a daring display of agility and strength.

The sport takes place at a cliff face near Heimaey's harbour. The cliff itself is called Sprangan, and the ledges have different names. These ledges provide the launching points for participants as they swing and leap to conquer the cliff face. The sport was originally developed by egg collectors, who would dangle themselves over the sheer cliffs every spring, swinging from side to side as they pilfered eggs from nests in the cliff. It turned into a competition between them, with the nimbler collectors completing daring twirls and tricks, until the island deemed it proper to hold a competition during the yearly festival (*see* p. 119) and initiate the few visitors to the island by letting them have a go themselves.

Spranga in action
Opposite **Hiking Kerlingarfjöll through Hveradalir**

THE HIGHLAND BASE

◉ KERLINGARFJÖLL

Located about one hour from Gullfoss along the Kjölur Route (*see* p. 54) are the mountains called Kerlingarfjöll. This group of pointed peaks are covered in ice year-round, the white snow melting slowly into the rusty orange mountains made through eruptions and the powerful hot springs that steam and belch in the valleys.

The area was historically used as a year-round skiing school, back when the mountains were covered in snow even at the height of summer. Over time, as the snow cover has dwindled, it's been turned into a hot spot for outdoor adventure and activity. Today, it's a hiking hot spot, with many travellers comparing it to Landmannalaugar.

The most popular place to visit in Kerlingarfjöll is the Hveradalir area. These mountains and valleys feature hiking trails that climb the spine of the hill above the sulphurous steam billowing in valleys below. About 3km (2 miles) back down the road is the Highland Base, a new luxury hotel located on the site of the former skiing school. It's an all-out luxurious stay for extended adventures in this geothermal area, with longer hikes available to several of the surrounding peaks.

KAYAKING AMONG ICEBERGS

⊙ HEINABERGSLÓN LAGOON

I watch as my guide, Óskar, powerfully paddles his kayak, heading straight for the iceberg in front of us. The nose crashes up onto the ice, and he swiftly and nimbly leaps out onto the ice, hauling the kayak behind him further out of the water. Turning to me, he motions for me to make my approach, and I nervously do the same. Paddling fast at the iceberg, a huge crunch greets me as my kayak lunges onto the ice. Óskar easily grabs the rope hanging from the front and hauls me up safely.

'This is the only lagoon where it's actually safe to walk on the icebergs,' says Óskar while we strap on some crampons to our boots. 'The icebergs here are wider at the bottom, meaning that they won't flip. The same can't be said of the icebergs at Jökulsárlón,' he muses. My mind leaps to stories of tourists jumping onto the icebergs at the glacier lagoon, completely unaware of the danger.

We're kayaking on the waters of Heinabergslón, a lagoon at the edge of the glacier Vatnajökull in the south-east of Iceland. While most people stop by the Jökulsárlón Glacier Lagoon, there are plenty more lagoons in this part of the country that aren't directly on the ring road, accessed via bumpy, rough tracks with minimal signs as to where they lead.

Óskar whips out a pickaxe, chipping away a set of impromptu stairs in the ice, leading us up into a small ice cave. Within, we can hear the water draining out from the iceberg to the lagoon beneath us. We paddle around the lagoon for the next three hours, venturing ever closer to the glacier tongue. Óskar picks out various icebergs to land on, where we crunch across the ice to admire ravines, ice caves and views of the surrounding landscape. At one point, we nose our kayaks underneath an overhang of ice, splashing through a curtain of water dripping off the edge to touch the ice with outstretched hands.

Heinabergslón is one of the several glacier lagoons in the region, with vast bodies of water emerging as the glacier tongues retreat. 'The glacier used to reach much further down than it does now. It takes about an hour to reach it in the kayaks now,' Óskar says. Before, he and his friends used to adventure onto the glacier in search of ice caves and ravines, or simply enjoy nature. 'I used to live in London, which was far too much,' he says. 'Then I moved to Reykjavík, and it was still too busy for me. I much prefer the quiet here.'

And quiet it is, letting us listen to the cry of a bird, the slosh of our paddles in the water and the slow creaking of the ice.

🔵 iceguide.is

Top **Kayaks rest alongside Heinabergslón Lagoon**

Bottom **Towering glaciers**

Top **Surfing on a black sand beach, outside of Vík**

Bottom **Adventurous surfers brave the Icelandic beaches**

SURFING THE ICY WATERS

◉ AROUND ICELAND

Icelanders are used to challenges. The early settlers who set sail from Norway were considered the most enterprising and adventurous people, and not much has changed. Although life is wonderfully comfortable for most in Iceland, there are still ways to seek out challenges, adversity and intense experiences.

The icy waters of the North Atlantic don't immediately come to mind when thinking of learning to surf – normally, if you picture surfing you'll see yourself in Hawaii or California, with palm trees swaying in a gentle breeze as you catch a perfect, glassy wave. Surfing in Iceland is a far different experience. There's most often a breeze, yes, but to call it gentle would be a misnomer, as the wind in Iceland is a far more forceful presence. Low-pressure systems that race across the North Atlantic collide with Iceland's intricate coastline, shaping swell into surfable waves across the country. Adventurous surfers can find surf breaking over jagged lava fields and massive rocks, but it's crucial to remember that unpredictable swell and weather patterns can be deadly.

That's why one of the pioneers of Iceland's surfing community, Ingó Olsen, began the company Arctic Surfers. Ingó and his friends have spent the last 20 years undertaking adventurous surfing expeditions, scouting out the best breaks in the country. The company offers a range of different tours. Beginners will want to join one of the surf school programs to learn the basics of surfing in Iceland. More experienced surfers can opt for a custom-made itinerary, where you'll venture into the furthest reaches of Iceland's coastline, seeking out the most epic swell and keying into the company's wide network of family and friends for a rugged adventure like no other.

🜂 arcticsurfers.com

MOUNTAINEERING & GLACIER SKILLS

⊙ AROUND ICELAND

Iceland is one of the best places in the world to train as a mountaineer, thanks in huge part to the varied and rugged landscapes. Honing your skills on the glaciers, volcanic mountains and everything in between gives you a fantastic foundation for taking your outdoor experience to the next level.

There are plenty of courses for travellers interested in learning the essential skills for navigating Iceland's landscapes. Several providers offer these programs to aspiring mountaineers, with courses ranging from beginner-friendly introductions to more advanced training.

For beginners, introductory courses provide a solid foundation of mountaineering skills not just for Iceland, but for anywhere else you might find yourself trekking through remote landscapes. The coursework covers topics like navigation, safety in the mountains, first aid and the use of essential gear like crampons and ice axes. All of this knowledge comes in handy if you're looking to explore Iceland's landscapes beyond the typical tourist routes or go on some of the country's long-distance hikes.

While setting foot on Iceland's glaciers without a guide is reserved for the most experienced adventurers, a glacier skills course is the first step towards becoming one yourself. Through hands-on experience in one of Iceland's most unique environments, you can pick up skills like crevasse rescue, rope skills and ice climbing, essential for anyone looking into a career as a glacier guide.

And for those craving serious adventures during Iceland's winter season? Winter skills are also taught in Iceland, covering everything from avalanche awareness to survival techniques in the snow. While most tourists in Iceland don't necessarily need these skills unless they are pursuing a career as an explorer or long-distance winter hiker, it's one of the more unique ideas to further your learning and experience a different side of Iceland.

🔘 mountainguides.is

🔘 bergmenn.com

🔘 northiceexpeditions.is

Top **Hiking on Svinafellsjökull Glacier**

Bottom **Equipment like harnesses, axes, crampons and helmets are essential on a glacier hike**

Hikers on the jaw-dropping
Laugavegur Trail

"From past to present, Þingvellir is the heart of the nation"

HISTORY

Top and bottom
**The Settlement Exhibition
in Reykjavík**

THE SETTLEMENT OF ICELAND

◉ REYKJAVÍK

Iceland was settled by Viking explorers in the late ninth century, sailing away from Norway after getting fed up with the king there and searching for a new life. Earlier explorers had discovered Iceland, and word spread of a beautiful and uninhabited country to the west. The future Icelanders set sail with their horses in tow, and after successive waves of immigration from Norway, much of the country was quickly divvied up into farmsteads. It's a story of daring exploration and harsh living conditions as the settlers adapted to their new home. For a full picture of Iceland's early history, there are a few essential stops on a trip.

The Settlement Center, Borgarnes

For a broad introduction to Iceland's settlement, this museum in Borgarnes is hard to beat. Located just over an hour north of Reykjavík, two restored warehouses on the town's shore visualise the early Vikings' journey sailing across the Atlantic, why they left Norway to begin with and the era from settlement until the creation of the world's first parliament at Þingvellir in 930 CE. A second exhibition recounts the adventures of Egil Skallagrímsson, the main star of one of Iceland's most exciting and wild Sagas, Egil's Saga.

The Settlement Exhibition, Reykjavík

Back in Reykjavík, the Settlement Exhibition is another interactive look at Iceland's early days. When a downtown hotel began renovating its basement, the remains of a Viking longhouse were discovered, which has now been turned into a museum detailing the first years of life for Vikings in Reykjavík. It was here that Iceland's first permanent settler, Ingólfur Arnarson, set up shop, and a wrap-around panoramic screen on the museum walls shows how things looked when this longhouse was in use. Also on display are other settlement-era finds from the area.

National Museum of Iceland, Reykjavík

The permanent exhibition 'Making of a Nation' at the National Museum of Iceland in the capital provides more context for Iceland's settlement. The exhibition details the early days of settlement through to the present day and includes over 2000 different artefacts from the country.

THE MEETING PLACE

⊙ ÞINGVELLIR NATIONAL PARK

Þingvellir National Park contains some spectacular natural scenery, but it's impossible to understate the area's importance in Icelandic history. When the first Vikings arrived in Iceland, they spread out around the country, claiming swathes of farmland for themselves and future generations. Keen to hang up their axes, they soon realised the importance of a structured society with common law. Gathering on the plains of Þingvellir in the year 930, the chieftains of the independent farms that made up Iceland decided to band together and create what is known as the first democratic parliament in the world, the Alþing.

The Alþing met once a year at Þingvellir, with an elected law speaker and chief in charge of settling disputes that arose throughout the year and crafting policy and laws. Here, farmers traded goods and gossip, announced marriages and made business deals. The gathering was the social event of the year, and even if there wasn't some big announcement taking place, attendees still found plenty of reasons to have a good time.

If, throughout the year, you had committed a heinous crime, you would be judged by your fellow countrymen, who decided whether you were to be banished from Iceland, executed or forced to duel for your life. When Christianity came to Iceland in the year 1000, it was here that the chieftains decided to adopt it as a nation, leaving the Norse religion and their old gods behind. It was also here that Iceland declared its independence from Denmark in 1944, with thousands gathering to witness the event. From past to present, Þingvellir is the heart of the nation, offering up not just a feast for the eyes, thanks to the tectonic rift, but a connection to the Icelandic people.

Phoenetic in Þingvellir

The thorn character þ is pronounced 'th', something to keep in mind when mentioning Þingvellir National Park to locals. The Icelandic alphabet contains 32 letters; you may have seen a few extra characters in the pages already. The character eth (Ð or ð) also makes a 'th' sound, although it's much softer than þ (your tongue should only touch the back, instead of the bottom, of your teeth), while Æ or æ sounds like the 'i' in ice.

Top **The tectonic plates at Þingvellir National Park meet underwater**

Bottom **Almannagjá gorge**

THE HERRING ERA MUSEUM

◉ SIGLUFJÖRÐUR

Arriving in Siglufjörður today, it's hard to imagine that this charming town was once Iceland's largest port, bustling with over 500 fishing boats and thousands of residents. It was herring that put Siglufjörður on the map. During the Great Depression and the subsequent war years, the global demand for canned food skyrocketed, and herring was the answer. Massive schools of these fish were abundant in the northern sea, bringing a tidal wave of prosperity to the town.

People from all over Iceland, Scandinavia and far beyond flocked to Siglufjörður, drawn by the promise of good money. The local population swelled to around 3000, and every summer, thousands more arrived in search of their share of the wealth that was being created. Dozens of languages were spoken in the streets, and the small town had the cosmopolitan feel of a much larger city. At its peak, herring exports made up around 25 per cent of Iceland's total exports. Historians agree that this economic boom was crucial in Iceland's push for independence in 1944.

Everything changed in the 1960s when the herring vanished overnight. Whether due to overfishing or changes in migration patterns, the fish completely disappeared, and within a few years, Siglufjörður was deserted, fading into a quiet memory. The once-bustling town turned into a quiet, forgotten place, the permanent population cut in half as locals left to find work in the capital. It remained like that for some time, until a revival of sorts with the increase in tourism to Iceland. Still, the place can feel a bit like a dream sequence, with empty houses and a town much larger than it needs to be for the small population.

Today, the story of Iceland's golden age of herring is vividly recounted at the Herring Era Museum. Even if you think you have no interest in fish, this museum is a must-visit. It features restored dormitories where seasonal workers slept, collections of their belongings discovered during renovations, all kinds of gear and even boats and a salting station. The museum paints a captivating picture of a bygone era that was hugely important in Iceland's history.

🌐 sild.is

SNORRASTOFA MUSEUM

⊙ BORGARFJÖRÐUR, WEST ICELAND

In the Borgarfjörður district of West Iceland, the Snorrastofa Museum at Reykholt invites visitors into the world of Snorri Sturluson, a pivotal figure in medieval Iceland and one of the country's great writers. Snorri, born in 1179, was a poet, historian and politician, and is most famous for penning the 'Prose Edda' and 'Heimskringla', two essential texts for understanding Norse mythology and the Sagas of the Norse kings.

Raised in the influential Sturlungar clan and educated at Oddi, Snorri's intellect and literary talent flourished when he was a boy. As an adult, his life was marred by the turbulent politics of the time; it was during the 13th century when Iceland was rife with power struggles between different clans. Snorri's involvement in these conflicts, particularly his shifting allegiance with King Hákon of Norway, eventually led to his assassination.

On the night of 23 September 1241, Snorri was killed in his home at Reykholt by men led by Gissur Þorvaldsson, a rival chieftain, on orders from King Hákon of Norway. Snorri's last words were *Eigi skal höggva!* (Do not strike!).

Today, Snorrastofa is a place for history and literature buffs; the farm has become a museum exploring Snorri's legacy through exhibits on his literary contributions and political life. Highlights include the ancient manuscripts, the underground tunnel where Snorri was assassinated and the reconstructed hot spring bath called Snorralaug, where Snorri used to bathe in the geothermal water (no swimming allowed). The museum also serves as a cultural event space and frequently hosts workshops and exhibitions.

🔗 snorrastofa.is

Top and opposite top **The historic Herring Era Museum**

Opposite bottom and previous **Snorrastofa Museum**

Top **The Helm of Awe or Helm of Terror, a Norse mythology symbol**

Bottom **Odin, the supreme god of Norse mythology**

ICELANDIC NAMING TRADITIONS

⊙ ICELANDIC EMIGRATION CENTER, HOFSÓS

Icelandic people do not have surnames in the traditional sense. Instead, the Vikings adopted a system where children were given their father's first name as a second name. It's also conjugated with the suffix *-son* (son) or *-dóttir* (daughter). A girl named Katla with a father called Sigurður becomes Katla Sigurðardóttir. And if Katla were to have a brother named Ragnar, his full name would be Ragnar Sigurðarson.

When it comes to first names, the Icelandic Naming Committee maintains a register with all the approved names. When a child is born in Iceland, only one of these approved names can be chosen. Icelanders can petition for a new name to be added to the list, but ultimately, it's up to the Naming Committee whether it will be accepted. Now and again, a news article will come out with a list of newly approved names – and those that were rejected. The Naming Committee keeps their register of approved names up to date and online for Icelanders to consult.

These Icelandic first names come from all over. Some are based on Norse mythology, while others are from characters or objects from the Sagas. Some names relate to famous saints, while others are the words for things found in Icelandic nature, like the sun, glacier, ocean or even some volcanoes. It's common for parents in Iceland to wait up to six months after the birth to reveal their baby's name. The name reveal is a big deal, and there's often a party involved with family and friends.

But why is there such strict control around Icelandic names? Any name submitted to the Naming Committee will be judged for its compatibility with Icelandic tradition, and whether it will cause the person any embarrassment. Common English names like Chris, Ben or Rebecca are swiftly rejected, as are any names that contain characters outside the Icelandic alphabet.

There are some descendants of Icelanders, though, whose names might have changed over time. During the 19th and 20th centuries, there was a large wave of emigration from Iceland due to harsh living conditions of the time, poverty and excessive natural disasters. North America in particular was a popular destination, and areas of Manitoba earned the nickname 'New Iceland'. The Icelandic Emigration Center (Vesturfarasetrið á Hofsósi) located in the small town of Hofsós in North Iceland is dedicated to emigration. Those who might have Icelandic names within their family tree could have a connection to these Icelanders who left in search of new opportunities, and the centre serves as not just a museum, but also a resource for those looking to trace their Icelandic ancestry through their extensive and thorough genealogical research.

⊘ hofsos.is

1238 – THE BATTLE OF ICELAND

⊙ SAUÐÁRKRÓKUR

Slipping on the virtual reality headset, I dive head-first into the bloodiest battle in Iceland's history. Things start quietly; I'm surrounded by other Vikings in a camp, everyone waking up slowly and beginning to polish their weapons. Today, we're set to do battle with an opposing Viking clan, vying for control of the region, and my fellow Vikings are sharpening their swords in anticipation.

But before we have too much time to react, a scout cries out that we're under attack; it's an unexpected ambush from the rival Viking clans. Before too long, I'm hurling spears and rocks as the largest battle that has ever taken place in Icelandic history rages around me.

This is the premise behind the interactive museum, 1238 – the Battle of Iceland. Located in Sauðárkrókur in the north, it's a part of Iceland that's pleasantly green, filled with working farms, gentle countryside and without huge-hitting attractions to make it too busy with tourists. But it wasn't always so peaceful, as I quickly find out.

The Battle of Örlygsstaðir occurred at the tail end of what's known as the Sturlung Era, a period of civil unrest in Iceland when powerful chieftain families vied for control of the country. I'm a part of the Sturlung Clan, but we can't rewrite history; slowly, our defences are overcome in the battle, my spears and rocks counting for nothing, my allies falling around me before, finally, our rivals kill my clan leader.

I take my cue and remove the VR headset, delivered once again back into peace and quiet. The weakened state of the Sturlung family after their defeat and the resulting power vacuum made it easy for Norway to intervene in Iceland's affairs. By 1262, Iceland had fallen under Norwegian rule, marking the end of Iceland's independence; it was only regained in 1944 (*see p. 112*).

1238 – The Battle of Iceland might just be one of the most interesting interactive museums in the country. You can also dress up in Viking costumes for photos and engage with more typical museum displays recounting the history of the bloody Sturlung Era.

🔗 1238.is

Top **Interactive exhibitions on the Battle of Örlygsstaðir**
Bottom **1238 – The Battle of Iceland**

169

Top **Austurvöllur Square is a symbol of the power of people's protest**

Bottom **Aerial view of Austurvöllur Square**

THE POTS & PANS REVOLUTION

⊙ AUSTURVÖLLUR SQUARE, REYKJAVÍK

The Pots and Pans Revolution was a defining moment in Icelandic history. During the 2008 Global Financial Crisis, Iceland's major banks collapsed under the weight of their massive debts. The small island nation was left teetering on the edge of bankruptcy, with ordinary Icelanders facing soaring loan repayments, a plummeting currency and widespread financial ruin. People lost their savings overnight, and a considerable number of businesses went completely under.

During this time, the country underwent a sort of revolution. Thousands of Icelanders took to the streets of Reykjavík, armed with pots, pans and other kitchen utensils, crashing them together to create a clattering symphony of banging metal. Demonstrators gathered outside the parliament building in Austurvöllur Square, demanding the resignation of government officials and the prosecution of the bank executives they held responsible for the financial catastrophe.

The pots and pans symbolised the ordinary Icelanders' struggle, and the event's impact was profound. By January 2009, the pressure culminated in the resignation of Prime Minister Geir Haarde and his government, leading to new elections and significant political reforms. Bank executives also faced prosecution and were found guilty of various charges including market manipulation, embezzlement and breach of fiduciary duty. These prosecutions resulted in significant jail time for many and extensive bans from operating in finance again.

This immediate political change at the hands of ordinary Icelanders empowered the country. Visitors to Iceland are often impressed by the country's rigorous approach to prosecuting bankers, as the scale of prosecution and severity of the penalties were seen as inadequate in most other nations.

To visit the site of this important moment in Icelandic history, head to Austurvöllur Square. Today, Icelanders still gather here to protest government policy and enact change.

THE NORDIC GAMBIT – CHESS IN ICELAND

⊙ GRÍMSEY ISLAND

Spend enough time in Iceland and someone somewhere will eventually bring up the 'Match of the Century,' a chess game between American Bobby Fischer and Russian Boris Spassky that took place in Reykjavík in 1972. Taking place at the height of the Cold War, the match mirrored the international tension of the time. Eventually, Bobby Fischer would beat his grandmaster opponent, ending 25 years of victories by the Russians. The match had a lasting impact on Iceland when it came to chess.

One place in Iceland has long been known as a holdout of chess: Grímsey Island (see p. 47). This isolated outpost straddling the Arctic Circle above Iceland is an odd place to be considered one of the hubs of chess in the country, but the Islanders are renowned for their proficiency in the game.

The long and dark winters on the island mean the locals have a lot of time to entertain themselves, and chess has become a popular game.

This fact was brought to the attention of a travelling professor Daniel Willard Fiske, who discovered Grímsey's love of chess as he sailed past. Grímsey's unique culture clearly left a mark on the professor. When he inherited a fortune from his late wife, he gifted the island with a library and 12 marble chessboards – one for each family living on Grímsey at the time, and one extra. These chessboards became cherished family heirlooms, passed down through generations.

If you visit Grímsey, make sure you visit the island's library, where the chessboards are kept. And if you challenge a local to a match? Prepare to get roundly beaten.

WOMEN & EQUALITY IN ICELAND

◉ **AROUND ICELAND**

Iceland isn't just known for its fascinating landscapes and Viking history; it's also the country that tops the World Economic Forum's Global Gender Gap Index. In other words, this is the top country in the world when it comes to gender equality. It has long been a country that has worked towards equality; on 24 October 1975, 90 per cent of Icelandic women went on strike to show how much society depended on women's labour. It was a pivotal moment in history for Icelandic women, who took a day off from their jobs and any housework. Iceland's economy was paralysed for a day, and the next day, local papers ran stories about men who had to do dishes for the first time and how stores ran out of hot dogs as fathers scrambled to feed hungry kids.

As a result of the strike, Iceland adopted its first Gender Equality Act the next year, in 1976, banning wage discrimination based on gender. The event also set the stage for the election of Vigdís Finnbogadóttir, the first woman in the world to be democratically elected as head of state. Since then, Icelandic women have gone on strike several more times, and each time it sparks debates, discussions and an overall stronger awareness among men of the challenges women face.

Today, Iceland enjoys a robust parental leave policy where both parents are entitled to equal leave, promoting shared responsibilities at home and supporting women's participation in the workforce. Additionally, Iceland enforces gender quotas for corporate boards and laws to help mitigate the gender wage gap – although it still exists. Iceland's parliament also has had the highest percentage of women anywhere in the world, ensuring that women's voices are integral to shaping policies that support gender equality.

While Iceland is a wonderful place to be a woman, gender disparities still need to be addressed. This was brought to the attention of the wider country in 2024, when Icelandic women went on strike again. Some 25,000 women gathered in Reykjavik to protest, the largest since the 'Women's Day Off' back in 1975.

Top **Vigdís Finnbogadóttir, the fourth president of Iceland**

Opposite top **Bobby Fischer and Boris Spassky face off**

Opposite bottom **Chess is hugely popular on Grímsey Island**

THE ERUPTION OF ELDFELL

⊙ HEIMAEY

Apart from the 2010 eruption of Eyjafjallajökull, one other volcanic eruption occurred in Iceland and garnered worldwide attention: the Eldfell eruption of 1973.

In the early hours of the morning on 23 January, residents of Heimaey awoke to sirens blaring. Awaiting them when they went to their windows and doors to see what was happening was a terrifying sight: a fissure had opened east of town and was spewing lava 150m (490ft) into the air.

What happened next has long been one of Iceland's most inspiring stories. A winter storm the previous day meant that the island's ships were safely moored in the harbour, and residents made their way down to the port for evacuation. As they sailed out of the harbour, they watched, with both horror and fascination, as rescue workers pumped seawater onto the approaching lava threatening to close their only exit.

Over 5000 people were evacuated in the night, and not one life was lost. Two days later, the lava had formed a 200m (656ft) cinder cone, spewing out even more lava and ash. The eruption would continue for the next five months, swallowing some 400 homes. Some residents would choose never to return.

The story of Eldfell's eruption illustrates the resilience of the Icelandic people but also underscores the precariousness of living above such immense power. Today, Heimaey is once again a thriving town, rebuilt but still in the shadows of the volcano that emerged to tower above town. It's still very much active, its warmth palpable to those who hike to the top, where vents in the earth emit waves of heat from down below.

For more information about the Eldfell eruption, visit the Eldheimar Museum (eldheimar.is) at the eastern edge of town.

A TIMELINE OF HISTORIC VOLCANIC ERUPTIONS IN ICELAND

1104 – Hekla Eruption, South Iceland

The 1104 eruption of Hekla, one of Iceland's most active volcanoes, was its largest recorded eruption. This explosive event produced massive ashfalls that blanketed farms and settlements, causing extensive damage and influencing Icelandic mythology and folklore.

1362 – Öræfajökull Eruption, South Iceland

The eruption of Öræfajökull in 1362 was among the most powerful eruptions in Iceland's history. It destroyed the district of Litlahérað, killing many people and leading to the area's renaming as Öræfi, meaning 'wasteland'.

1783 – Laki Eruption, South Iceland

The Laki fissure eruption of 1783 was one of the largest volcanic events in recorded history, releasing vast amounts of lava and toxic gases over an eight-month period. This catastrophic event led to widespread famine and disease in Iceland, killing about a quarter of the population and affecting climate and agriculture across Europe.

1875 – Askja Eruption, Eastern Highlands

The 1875 Askja eruption in the Eastern Highlands expelled massive amounts of ash, impacting large parts of Iceland and other places as far away as Scandinavia. This eruption caused significant agricultural damage and led to a wave of emigration from Iceland.

1918 – Katla Eruption, South Iceland

The 1918 Katla eruption produced vast amounts of ash and glacial meltwater floods, known as *jökulhlaup*. This eruption extended Iceland's southern coastline and caused significant damage to local farmlands and infrastructure.

1973 – Eldfell, Westman Islands

The eruption of Eldfell in 1973 on Vestmannaeyjar (the Westman Islands) began unexpectedly and led to the evacuation of the entire population of Heimaey. The eruption buried homes in lava and ash and forever changed the idea of security on the island – a reminder of the volatile forces of nature at play in Iceland.

2010 – Eyjafjallajökull, South Iceland

The 2010 Eyjafjallajökull eruption caused widespread disruption due to the massive ash cloud that grounded air traffic across Europe for several days. This eruption highlighted the global impact of Iceland's volcanic activity and led to a huge increase of interest in Iceland as a tourist destination.

The effects of Eldfell's eruption in 1973

A volcanic eruption in 2010

"Even the untrained eye will notice trolls turned to stone by the rising sun, the faces of giants in mountains and caves"

ART & CULTURE

NATIONAL GALLERY OF ICELAND

⊙ REYKJAVÍK

Often overlooked for other museums in the capital, the National Gallery of Iceland packs a decent punch when it comes to Icelandic art. Occupying a former ice store, in which blocks of ice carved out of the pond Tjörnin were stored, here you'll find the best collection of works by Icelandic artists. There are plenty of landscapes that you might recognise from your journey around Iceland, depictions of the famous Sagas and temporary exhibitions that mainly focus on modern-day Icelandic artists.

ARTIST RESIDENCIES IN ICELAND

Iceland has long been a magnet for artists looking to find inspiration in the remote landscapes and unique culture. Here are five residencies around the country to consider if you're looking for a place to create.

Gröndal's House Residency, Reykjavík

A writer's residency inside Gröndalshús in downtown Reykjavík, the restored former residence of the renowned Icelandic writer, illustrator and scholar Benedikt Gröndal (1826–1907).

The Freezer Residency, Snæfellsbær, West Iceland

Residency for theatre makers, performance artists, dancers and musicians at the Freezer Hostel in Hellissandur, occupying a former fish factory.

The Westfjords Residency, Þingeyri, Westfjords

Residency for artists of various disciplines in Þingeyri, a village in the Westfjords. Run by the couple who own the local cafe, Simbahöllin. Open seasonally.

Fish Factory Creative Centre, Stöðvarfjörður, East Iceland

Residency for artists of various disciplines in a renovated fish factory in the small town of Stöðvarfjörður in the Eastfjords.

Old School Art House, Hrísey Island, North Iceland

This artist residency is located inside a home on the island of Hrísey, in the middle of Eyjafjörður in North Iceland. Remote and quiet, and ideal for various disciplines.

Bottom **The National Gallery of Iceland has the best collection of Icelandic art**

Opposite **A sculpture by Sigurjón Ólafsson greets visitors**

Tvísöngur sound sculpture

ART & SOUND

⊙ TVÍSÖNGUR, SEYÐISFJÖRÐUR

Perched on a mountainside above Seyðisfjörður, the Tvísöngur sound sculpture is a strange piece of architecture. Created by German artist Lukas Kühne, from afar, the collection of concrete domes looks like interconnected mushrooms. But it's inside where the magic happens.

Tvísöngur is composed of five interconnected domes, each ranging in height from 2m (6.5ft) to 4m (13ft). Covering an area of about 30 sqm (323 sq ft), this unique installation is a tribute to the Icelandic musical tradition of five-tone harmony. This form of music is deeply rooted in Icelandic culture and tradition, and each of the five domes that make up Tvísöngur is designed to resonate with one of the five specific tones.

What this means is that as the wind blows through the openings of the domes, it interacts with the structure to produce sounds that reflect those five tones. Standing inside is like experiencing the wind itself playing a giant instrument, the melody deeply tied to Icelandic tradition. The acoustics are also fantastic, and the site has been the location of live music performances since its inception.

This rare blend of architecture, art and acoustics is ideally located; Seyðisfjörður has a strong reputation within Iceland as a bit of an artsy hub. Each summer, it hosts the LungA festival (lunga.is), an intimate art festival that celebrates creativity, arts and culture, with a week-long schedule of workshops, lectures and events.

THE OLD HERRING FACTORY

⊙ DJÚPAVÍK, STRANDIR COAST

In the summer of 2006, Sigur Rós, one of Iceland's most celebrated bands, embarked on a two-week tour across their homeland. Their journey took them to unique locations across the country, from places like Ásbyrgi Canyon in the north to outdoor stages in small fishing villages like Ólafsvík, with each performance captured in their acclaimed documentary *Heima*. The film premiered at the Reykjavík Film Festival in 2007 and quickly garnered a cult following.

One performance stood out: a concert in an abandoned herring factory in Djúpavík, a remote town on the Strandir Coast. Playing to an intimate crowd of 300, the band's ethereal music echoed through the industrial ruins, creating a mesmerising experience. This event transformed the factory into a pilgrimage site for fans keen to discover the spooky ruins of what was once Iceland's largest herring factory.

Icelanders saw potential for the space to be reborn as a cultural hub. Since 2015, the Djúpavík Hotel has hosted The Factory, an annual festival that fills the abandoned factory with site-specific art, installations and sound displays. The rusting factory, set against the backdrop of contemporary art installations that fill each space, creates an eerie yet captivating atmosphere.

Visitors can explore the factory's interior, now home to a diverse collection of art that changes every year. It's the country's most unique fusion of history, music and art, and makes the Old Herring Factory a must-visit for art lovers in Iceland.

Top **Inside the abandoned factory**
Bottom **The Old Herring Factory has become the setting for an annual art festival**

Top and bottom **Huldufólk houses camouflaged in the landscape**

THE ICELANDIC HULDUFÓLK

◉ REYKJAVÍK

Iceland is a place that can cast a strange spell upon even the most practical of minds. Consider the northern lights and midnight sun, the twisted lava fields and mist-covered mountains, the moss and fierce winds – these wonders can all feed the imagination.

Icelanders have spent over 1000 years living alongside these sounds, shapes and surreal landscapes, and a strong culture around the supernatural has grown from that lived experience. You might scoff, but even the untrained eye will notice trolls turned to stone by the rising sun, the faces of giants in mountains and caves and roads that inexplicably skirt otherwise ordinary-looking boulders.

Exploring Iceland's rich folklore adds another layer to an already captivating culture. A parallel spiritual realm inhabited by the Huldufólk, or 'hidden people', exists across the entire country. These supernatural beings are invisible to the human eye and live in the rocks, canyons and other special locations. There's an abundance of stories and legends surrounding Iceland's Huldufólk; for example, it's said that if you sit naked at a crossroads at midnight on the summer solstice, the Huldufólk might appear bearing gifts and riches for you. Other stories tell of bulldozers and tractors being damaged overnight after altering a certain landscape and offending them. The list goes on.

Apart from the Huldufólk, there are also trolls, giants, spiritual beings, ghosts and even zombies. Few know that JRR Tolkien wrote his thesis on Old Iceland and the folklore directly influenced *The Lord of the Rings*.

To learn more about the Icelandic Huldufólk and folklore in general, a folklore walking tour in Reykjavík is a suitable place to start; see yourfriendinReykjavik.com for more information.

"For locals, it's a strong reminder of the tenacity and adaptability of their ancestors"

ARCHITECTURE

HALLGRÍMSKIRKJA, THE CHURCH OF BASALT

⦿ AROUND ICELAND

The imposing grey tower of Hallgrímskirkja dominates the Reykjavík skyline, the city's most prominent landmark and source of national pride. At 74m (243ft) tall and perched atop one of the highest hills of the capital, you can see the church from 25km (15.5 miles) away. It draws you up the long street of Skólavörðustígur to stand beneath its towering presence. Designed by Guðjón Samúelsson, Iceland's former state architect, it pays homage to the basalt columns formed by cooling lava around Iceland – art forms found in nature. To admire the inspiration yourself, head to one of the following locations around Iceland.

Reynisfjara Black-Sand Beach, South Iceland

Iceland's most famous black-sand beach is Reynisfjara, sitting on the south coast in the shadow of the glaciers Eyjafjallajökull and Mýrdalsjökull. A wall of basalt cliffs rises from the sand at one side, twisting into caves along the shore and providing some prime nesting spots for puffins in the summer.

Kirkjugólf, Kirkjubæjarklaustur, South Iceland

Outside a former church you'll find a floor of hexagonal basalt columns. This was created in 1783 when nearby Laki erupted, sending sulphur and ash raining down from the sky. After months of eruptions lava began to seep into Kirkjubæjarklaustur. The local pastor, Jón Steingrímsson, gathered his congregation inside the church, giving what is now known as the Eldmessa ('fire sermon'), where he reproached the crowd for their sins and laziness. He made a believer out of all of them when the lava stopped right at the edge of the church – forming today what you can see as Kirkjugólf.

Svartifoss Waterfall, Skaftafell, South-East Iceland

Combine the beautiful grey basalt columns with a picturesque waterfall, and you've got yourself Svartifoss, the star attraction of Skaftafell in south-east Iceland (see p. 37). It takes about 45 minutes to hike here from the Skaftafell Visitor Centre, and the postcard-perfect waterfall shooting over the black and grey basalt cliffs awaits you.

Stuðlagil Canyon, East Iceland

This canyon's twisting basalt columns were revealed when the Kárahnjúkar Dam was built upriver. The dam harnessed glacial water to power a nearby aluminium-smelting plant in Reyðarfjörður. When the dam was built, the river dropped in height, revealing the stunning cliffs on either side of the canyon.

Aldeyjarfoss Waterfall, North Iceland

An often-overlooked waterfall, Aldeyjarfoss is found on a bumpy F-Road heading inland from a stretch of the ring road in northern Iceland. On either side of this short but powerful cascade are beautiful basalt cliffs, a bit like Svartifoss.

Top and bottom **The notable exterior and interior of Hallgrímskirkja Church**

The basalt columns at Kirkjugólf, also known as 'the church floor'

Top **A historic turf house built into the countryside**

Bottom **Sænautasel turf house**

TO BUILD A HOME – TURF HOUSES OF ICELAND

📍 **AROUND ICELAND**

While today Iceland is a modern and trendy tourist hub, it wasn't so long ago that most of the population lived in turf houses. Ask around, and you'll quickly find someone whose grandparents lived in a turf house – the last known occupancy inside these living, breathing relics of Icelandic history was in 1992. Offering far better insulation than buildings made entirely from stones or wood, these homes were key to surviving Iceland's harsh climate in the early days of settlement.

To build a turf house, a base layer of flat stones was put in place for a foundation, upon which the frame was erected, made from either birch or driftwood. Then, the entire structure was covered in several layers of turf, which would continue to grow and fuse together, helping to make the structure stronger and more weather-resistant over time. Turf houses were built individually but usually placed next to other turf houses, creating complexes connected by passageways in which the innermost rooms retained the most warmth and acted as the main living quarters – or *baðstofa* in Icelandic.

Travelling Iceland today, you'll still see great examples of these turf homes dotted around the landscape, painting a picture of what Iceland was like before tourism arrived. And for locals, it's a strong reminder of the tenacity and adaptability of their ancestors.

For the best examples of turf houses in Iceland, Glaumbær in the north-west is hard to beat. There's also Laufás in the north just outside of Akureyri, or the turf houses that are a part of the Skógar Museum in South Iceland.

HARPA CONCERT & CONFERENCE HALL

⦿ REYKJAVÍK

Harpa Concert and Conference Hall is Iceland's most modern and striking architectural icon. Designed by Henning Larsen and Batteríið Architects, in collaboration with multidisciplinary Icelandic artist Ólafur Elíasson, the building is a tribute to Iceland's dramatic landscape.

The structure resembles a mountain-like massif, perched on the water's edge with clear views of the sea and mountains across the fjord. The iconic geometric facade is inspired by the basalt cliffs found around the country, and the crystalline glass reflects the changeable Icelandic light throughout the day. The design brings together the city with the sea and mountains, underlining Reykjavík's connection to nature.

Inside, visitors can wander around the different floors, admiring the views and the light as it reflects through the exterior. Harpa is home to the Iceland Symphony Orchestra and the Icelandic Opera and hosts events ranging from local school musicals to huge international comedy and music acts. One of the most popular shows for visitors to Iceland is the long-running How to Become Icelandic in 60 Minutes, a comedy show that teaches you how to walk, talk and behave like a regular Icelander.

The distinctive Harpa
Concert Hall

"Here you can forget the clock and instead pay attention to the changing of the tide and the bloom of the flowers"

SLOW MO TRAVEL

ICELAND'S FIRST DESIGNATED SLOW CITY

⊙ **DJÚPIVOGUR**

East Iceland's Djúpivogur is a quiet little town amid some huge landscapes. Jutting out on a peninsula between two fjords, it's a place that's open to the elements, but it's a small price to pay for the splendid views it enjoys, with mountain peaks sweeping quickly up from the sea. The panoramas are incredible, especially if you take them in from the highest point in the city, Búlandsnes, a rocky hill above town.

Djúpivogur is the first Icelandic destination to join the 'Cittaslow' movement, a collection of places worldwide dedicated to living a slow and enjoyable life. That means it's a place to slow down and enjoy a walk around the harbour or a stop by a cafe, and not just breeze through like so many do in this part of Iceland.

And it's when you slow down that you discover the beauty of this place. A walk along the coast brings you closest to the island offshore called Papey, named after the Irish monks who called it home before Iceland was settled (they were swiftly given the boot after the Vikings arrived). Today, it's flocked with puffins, seals and seabirds in the summer and home to the country's smallest church.

While there's no official way to get to the island, your chances are pretty good if you hang around for a while and chat with locals. Eventually, you'll run into someone with a boat at the harbour, who could be convinced to take you out for a closer look.

The bay of sleepy Djúpivogur

Djúpivogur is best
accessed by boat

Top **Travelling to Flatey**

Bottom **Flatey has a modest population that lives on the island**

OFF THE CLOCK IN BREIÐAFJÖRÐUR

⊙ FLATEY ISLAND

Located in the middle of Breiðafjörður, Flatey is the largest and only populated island in a clutch of low-lying islands and skerries. This is a place where the attraction lies in the simple beauty that surrounds you, from the colourful houses that dot the island to the long grass rippling in the breeze and the sound of the tide washing against the shore. Time on Flatey moves differently – if you alight from the ferry here you can forget the clock and instead pay attention to the changing of the tide and the bloom of the flowers to immerse yourself fully in the dream-like state that the long summer days bring. It's a destination far removed from the frantic rush around the ring road and the busyness of Iceland's most famous natural attractions.

Settled early in the 10th century, Flatey became a centre of learning and research when an Augustinian monastery was built on the island in 1172. It remained that way until the German Hanseatic League showed up in the 16th century to begin trading, quickly making the island one of the wealthier places in Iceland. It boomed again in the 19th century, thanks to fishing, and during that time, hundreds of fishermen and their families called Flatey home. Things only died down after the world wars when the islanders left for Reykjavík. Today, only a few families remain on the island year-round, although during summer plenty of people return to while away the hazy summer days in this picturesque spot.

To visit, catch the ferry from the port in Stykkishólmur on the Snæfellsnes Peninsula. You'll soon find yourself braced against the rails, admiring birdlife and looking for whales as the ferry plods through the thousands of islands that dot Breiðafjörður. Spend the night at the humble island hotel, offering comfortable Scandinavian-style rooms spread across several 19th-century homes and a cosy restaurant.

WELLNESS AT ICELAND'S LUXURIOUS HOT SPRINGS

⊙ AROUND ICELAND

Iceland's abundance of geothermal power means that hot water bubbles up all over the country. There are swimming pools in almost every town in the country, while more natural hot springs (*see p. 44*) make for nice spots for a soak in the outdoors. And then there are the more luxurious hot springs, catering to a growing trend of wellness travellers looking to Iceland for its heavenly hot waters. The two most famous are, of course, the Blue Lagoon and the Mývatn Nature Baths; however, avoid the crowds at one of the following spots instead.

Hvammsvík Hot Springs, Hvalfjörður

This is a gorgeous spot on the shores of Hvalfjörður, a large fjord to the north of Reykjavík. What used to be a small hot spring on private land has turned into a large complex, with eight pools on the shore providing views of the sea and mountains.

🔗 hvammsvik.com

The Forest Lagoon, Akureyri

Akureyri in North Iceland is one of the few places in Iceland with a substantial forest – soil erosion due to wind and sapling-eating sheep have made it hard to grow trees here since the Vikings chopped them all down for fuel and shelter. The Forest Lagoon is exactly what it sounds like – a dreamy hot spring underneath a canopy of trees, with views over Eyjafjörður toward Akureyri.

🔗 forestlagoon.is

Geosea Baths, Húsavík

Perched at the edge of the cliffs above Húsavík in North Iceland, the infinity pools of Geosea Baths offer uninterrupted views over the stunning Skjálfandi Bay. This is Iceland's hot spot for whale watching (*see p. 67*), so keep your eyes peeled while you enjoy a soak.

🔗 geosea.is

Vök Baths, Egilsstaðir

East Iceland has one of the finest hot springs in the country, created when locals discovered a small patch of water on a lake that never froze over. Turns out there was geothermal water bubbling up from the bottom of the lake, which has now been channelled into lovely hot springs set out over the lake.

🔗 vokbaths.is

Laugarvatn Fontana, Golden Circle

Despite its great location smack bang in the middle of the Golden Circle, Laugarvatn Fontana remains a quiet and relaxing experience for those looking for a dose of wellness. Lava rocks surround the various pools and hot tubs, and a nearby pier leads out over the lake if you fancy a cold plunge. It also runs tours to a nearby geothermal bakery, where they bake bread underground using natural geothermal sources.

🔗 fontana.is

Top **The scenic Geosea Baths in Húsavík**

Bottom **Vök Baths in winter**

INDEX

The Icelandic character þ (thorn) falls after y in the Icelandic alphabet, so we have honoured this order in our index. Something to keep in mind if you find yourself alphabetising in Iceland.

ABOUT THE AUTHOR

James Taylor is an Australian travel writer who has spent the past decade living in Europe. Ever since setting foot in Iceland he knew that the country was something special. Even though he doesn't call the country home any more, he returns regularly for work, travel and ensuring his half-Icelandic son learns the language from his wife's side of the family.

Published in 2025 by Hardie Grant Explore,
an imprint of Hardie Grant Publishing

Hardie Grant Explore (Melbourne)
Wurundjeri Country
Level 11, 36 Wellington Street
Collingwood VIC 3066

Hardie Grant Explore (Sydney)
Gadigal Country
Level 7, 45 Jones Street
Ultimo, NSW 2007

hardiegrant.com/explore

The maps in this publication incorporate data from the
following sources:
Data from OpenStreetMap www.openstreetmap.org/
copyright, OpenStreetMap is open data, licensed under
the Open Data Commons Open Database License
(ODbL) by the OpenStreetMap Foundation (OSMF).
https://opendatacommons.org/licenses/odbl/1-0/
Any rights in individual contents of the database are
licensed under the Database Contents License:
https://opendatacommons.org/licenses/dbcl/1-0/
Data extracts via Geofabrik GmbH
https://www.geofabrik.de

Made with Natural Earth. Free vector and raster map
data @ naturalearthdata.com.

A catalogue record for this
book is available from the
National Library of Australia

Hardie Grant acknowledges the Traditional Owners of
the Country on which we work, the Wurundjeri People
of the Kulin Nation and the Gadigal People of the Eora
Nation, and recognises their continuing connection to
the land, waters and culture. We pay our respects to
their Elders past and present.

Intrepid Iceland
ISBN 9781741179330

10 9 8 7 6 5 4 3 2 1

Publisher
Megan Cuthbert

Editor
Monique Choy

Editorial assistance
Siena O'Kelly

Proofreader
Lyric Dodson

Cartographer
Emily Maffei

Design
George Saad Studios

Typesetting
Megan Ellis

Index
Max McMaster

Production manager
Simone Wall

Colour reproduction and pre-press by Megan Ellis
and Splitting Image Colour Studio

Printed and bound in China by LEO Paper Products LTD.

The paper this book is printed on
is certified against the Forest
Stewardship Council® Standards
and other sources. FSC® promotes
environmentally responsible, socially
beneficial and economically viable
management of the world's forests.

Disclaimer: While every care is taken to ensure the
accuracy of the data within this product, the owners of
the data do not make any representations or warranties
about its accuracy, reliability, completeness or suitability
for any particular purpose and, to the extent permitted
by law, the owners of the data disclaim all responsibility
and all liability (including without limitation, liability
in negligence) for all expenses, losses, damages
(including indirect or consequential damages) and costs
which might be incurred as a result of the data being
inaccurate or incomplete in any way and for any reason.

Publisher's Disclaimers: The publisher cannot
accept responsibility for any errors or omissions. The
representation on the maps of any road or track is
not necessarily evidence of public right of way. The
publisher cannot be held responsible for any injury, loss
or damage incurred during travel. It is vital to research
any proposed trip thoroughly and seek the advice of
relevant state and travel organisations before you leave.

Publisher's Note: Every effort has been made to ensure
that the information in this book is accurate at the time
of going to press. The publisher welcomes information
and suggestions for correction or improvement.